To Wr...
Hope this inspires
JO.

BUS·NESS
GEN!US

BUS•NESS
GEN!US

Deceptively simple ways to sharpen your business thinking

James Bannerman

PEARSON

Harlow, England • London • New York • Boston • San Francisco • Toronto • Sydney
Auckland • Singapore • Hong Kong • Tokyo • Seoul • Taipei • New Delhi
Cape Town • São Paulo • Mexico City • Madrid • Amsterdam • Munich • Paris • Milan

Pearson Education Limited
Edinburgh Gate
Harlow CM20 2JE
United Kingdom
Tel: +44 (0)1279 623623
Web: www.pearson.com/uk

First published 2014 (print and electronic)

© James Bannerman 2014 (print and electronic)

The right of James Bannerman to be identified as author of this work has been asserted by him in accordance with the Copyright, Designs and Patents Act 1988.

Pearson Education is not responsible for the content of third-party internet sites.

ISBN: 978-1-292-01266-7 (print)
        978-1-292-01268-1 (PDF)
        978-1-292-01269-8 (ePub)
        978-1-292-01267-4 (eText)

British Library Cataloguing-in-Publication Data
A catalogue record for the print edition is available from the British Library

Library of Congress Cataloging-in-Publication Data
Bannerman, James.
  Business genius : deceptively simple ways to sharpen your business thinking / James Bannerman.
    pages cm
  ISBN 978-1-292-01266-7 (limp)
  1. Creative ability in business. 2. Creative thinking. 3. Management. I. Title.
  HD53.B36 2014
  650.1--dc23
                          2014031002

ARP impression 98

Text design by Design Deluxe
Cover design by David Carroll & Co

Print edition typeset in 9.5pt Helvetica by 30
Printed in Great Britain by Ashford Colour Press Ltd

NOTE THAT ANY PAGE CROSS REFERENCES REFER TO THE PRINT EDITION

Dedicated to my mother – Elizabeth Monica Bannerman (1935–2011) – who helped me to appreciate people's unlimited potential

And to A, T and S xxx

CONTENTS

 Part 1 Improve yourself

 Part 2 Get on with others

Part 3 Achieve in business

ACKNOWLEDGEMENTS

Firstly, I'd like to thank Tony Buzan whose uplifting words of guidance, and encouragement, inspired me to write this book.

Secondly, I'd like to thank Eloise Cook, Lucy Carter, Paul East (and all the amazing Pearson team) for helping me to expand the **Genius** brand.

Thirdly, as always, I'd like to thank my department of business and management colleagues at Oxford Brookes University for their continued support and friendship. In particular: Richard Beresford, Nicolette Michels, Richard Mohun, Clive Wildish, Dr Karen Handley, Professor Phil James and Dr David Bowen. Added to this, I'd like to thank my external PhD supervisor Professor Fiona Patterson of Cambridge University, all the Warwick executive education team at WBS (especially Paul McCarthy, Kathleen Molan, Nick Barclay, Niki Latham and Elizabeth Bowkett) and Professor Graham Ward of INSEAD.

Finally, I'd also like to extend my gratitude to a rich variety of other people, for a million different reasons. These include: Tom Kenyon-Slaney, Harrienath Pillay (and all my excellent London Speaker Bureau contacts around the world), Don Taylor, Khoi Tu, Olly and Noni Needs, Charlie Beauchamp, Jon Callard, Hugh Griffiths, Julie Hay, John Barron,Tim Jones and Pippa Consadine, Jon and Hillary Stock, Jack and Finn Harries, Tony Henderson, Major-General Jonathan Shaw, Dilli Gurung, Philippa Thomas, Laura Whitworth, Jennifer Shipside, Chris Burton, Paddy Thompson, Letitia Blake, Sahera Chohan, Dom Weatherhead,

Julia Lee, Ben Mumby-Croft, Ian and Caroline Dunne, Ian Francis, John Thynne, James Lush, Ali Golds, Paul Sloane, MOK, Jon Black, Simon Jones, Thomas Power, Jane Hooper, Michael Spencer, Dr Mike Bagshaw, Andy Caughey, Joe Wengler, Ian Stevens, Professor John Adair, Professor Albert Bandura, Kristin Kulsavage, Adynah Johson, Oleg Lyubner and Joanna Beazley-Richards, whose far-reaching psychological insights (into why people do what they do) have proved invaluable.

And, of course, to my family and friends for always being there ...

ABOUT THE AUTHOR

James Bannerman
Creative change agent

James Bannerman is a creative change agent who combines creativity with psychology to help businesses innovate.

As an innovation consultant he has worked with many leading organisations including Aston Martin, Rolls-Royce, Starbucks, Balfour-Beatty, Atos Origin, SingTel and HSBC, as well as at the National Space Centre on a mission to Mars. He also lectures on business creativity and innovation on the MBA programmes at Warwick Business School, Grenoble Ecole de Management and Oxford Brookes University, where he is currently doing a PhD on the impact of lateral thinking on organisational performance.

Before working in business he was a platinum-selling songwriter, a freelance cartoonist (e.g. *Punch*), a trained clinical psychotherapist, and he has an MA in English literature from Edinburgh University.

AUTHOR'S NOTE

I used to think **Business Genius** was like the Crown Jewels: a treasure so precious, and rare, it was out of reach for most people ...

Now I'm not so sure.

Having worked with thousands of business leaders, managers and teams over the years (from world-famous companies like Aston Martin, British Airways, HSBC and Rolls-Royce to many public sector organisations and small start-ups, too) I've come to discover how virtually *all* of us can have **Genius** moments in the workplace from time to time. And, with a little help, we can have more.

Clearly, this doesn't mean we've all got what it takes to become:

→ the *next* Sir Richard Branson, whose entrepreneurial **Genius** (and 'flying in the face of ordinary thinking') helped Virgin expand into a multi-billion dollar empire;

- → the *next* Oprah Winfrey, whose media **Genius** helped her evolve into one of the top success stories in TV history; or

- → the *next* Steve Jobs (1955–2011) whose innovative **Genius** helped transform Apple into the world's No. 1 brand.

Fortunately, however, this book doesn't aim to turn you into the *next* anybody!

It simply aims to inspire you, and uplift you, with a variety of smart thinking strategies others have used to excel at work, so you are better placed to maximise your own **Business Genius** potential …

JcB.

INTRODUCTION

Excel! UP! your thinking, UP! your work, UP! your life

Most of us – if we're completely honest with ourselves – would love to take our working lives to new heights.

We'd love to **UP!** the way we feel about ourselves, **UP!** the way we get on with others, and **UP!** what we achieve in business …

And this is where this book is designed to help.

Business Gen!us will introduce you to a variety of innovative and insightful mind tools for enabling you to *soar* above the ordinary to reach the extraordinary.

With this in mind, each section will start by looking at a specific **B**lock and **L**imitation that can often hold us back and stifle our potential.

Then, more importantly, you'll be provided with some **U**seful tips and **E**scape strategies to *free* your **Genius** so you can rise above, and glide beyond, what's standing in your way.

And that's why it's no coincidence the cover of this book is **BLUE**.

Before we begin this *upwards and onwards* ascent, however, let's be brutally honest about one thing. At the end of the day:

'Our attitude determines our altitude.'

Stephen Covey (business leadership expert and author of *The 7 Habits of Highly Effective People*)

Coco Chanel, for example, could easily have thought, 'I don't have the resources to excel in business' (having grown up in the 1880s in a humble poorhouse in Saumur, France). But she didn't. As a result of her **Business Genius** attitude (or **UP!titude** as we call it) she went on to become the world-famous fashion designer we know today. Added to this, thanks to her amazing resourcefulness, Chanel No. 5 is now regarded as one of the best-known, and best-loved, perfumes of all time.

Similarly, Mark Zuckerberg could easily have thought, 'I'm too young to excel in business.' But he didn't. As a result of his **UP!titude**, the founder of Facebook became the youngest self-made billionaire in business history in 2007, at the age of only 23!

Or, consider Colonel Harland Sanders of Kentucky Fried Chicken fame. He could easily have thought, 'I'm too old to excel in business.' But he didn't. As a result of his **UP!titude**, the vintage entrepreneur (who, by this time was already in his mid-60s) massively boosted his tiny pension by franchising his secret recipe to food outlets across America.

So, whatever line of work you're in, and whatever improvements you're keen to make – from services to products, effectiveness to efficiency, or productivity to profitability – please be aware that **Business Genius** is ultimately linked to *the way* we think.

We'll cover this in more detail as we go.

Right now, however, let's be brutally honest about one other thing: the phrase '**Business Genius**' invariably means different things to different people (from wealth wizard to management guru) …

BUSINESS GEN!US…

Within the context of this book, however, it simply means this:

Smarter thinking, smarter working

Here are three different examples to highlight why:

1 BUSINESS GENIUS AND THE WORLD OF ARCHITECTURE

During the 1920s, the architect Albert Moore was asked to design a showcase building for OXO (the beef stock company) bang in the heart of London. But there was a problem.

Back then the City of London had strict advertising laws and was determined to prevent any company from drawing too much attention to itself.

So what did Moore do?

Well, instead of promoting OXO on large billboards or illuminated signs – which he knew would have been turned down, or pulled down, by the authorities – he decided to integrate the word OXO into the *brickwork* of the building itself!

Consequently, for anyone looking up at the windows of the Art Deco OXO Tower, the geometrical shapes of a circle on top of a cross on top of another circle looked ingeniously similar to the business name he wasn't *allowed* to make too noticeable.

What made Moore's approach even more of a stroke of **Business Genius**, however, was that years later – long after the building was sold off – it *still* continues to promote OXO on the South Bank of the River Thames. Why? Because the Tower became such an iconic landmark it's now registered as a grade II listed building, which means nobody can pull it down, even if they want to (without the appropriate legislation to do so). **Genius!**

2 BUSINESS GENIUS AND THE WORLD OF BASKETBALL

Many moons ago, in the USA, a group of Chicago basketball players – called the Savoy Big Five – impressed and entertained crowds with their amazing basketball tricks.

However, the challenge was that, although they were big (in terms of height), they weren't yet big (in terms of commercial success). And that's where the **Business Genius** of Abe Saperstein helped to make a big difference.

Saperstein recognised that talent alone isn't always enough in the big wide world of business. Consequently, he helped the Savoy Big Five to 'monetise' their talent by giving them a new look, and a new name, so they could appeal to a much bigger audience.

Firstly, he used smarter thinking, smarter working to rebrand their outfits (adopting the all-American colours of red, white and blue).

Secondly, he used smarter thinking, smarter working to come up with an ingenious brand name that sounded both distinctly African-American (Harlem) *and* internationally successful, too (Globetrotters).

Consequently, the Harlem Globetrotters rose to became 'the most famous basketball team in the world'. And, added to this, in 1971 the 5 ft 5 in Abe Saperstein became the smallest man ever to be inaugurated into the Basketball Hall of Fame!

3 BUSINESS GENIUS AND THE WORLD OF CARS

Forgive me if you know this example already (because it's been around for donkey's years), but its underlying message is as relevant as ever.

Back in the 1960s the car hire company Avis was, yet again, struggling to compete with its arch-rival Hertz. Hertz was the undisputed No. 1 in the marketplace, and not only had a much bigger fleet of cars but also had a much larger revenue to play around with. So what could they do?

Well, thanks to a flash of **Business Genius** inspiration – which took place when Avis's President Robert C. Townsend met up

with Paula Green and Helmut Krone of the ad agency DDB on Madison Avenue, New York – they used *smarter thinking, smarter working* to surpass this tricky problem.

Up until that point it was assumed that being No. 2 was naturally *inferior* to being No. 1. But then they started to *challenge this assumption* and *reverse this logic.*

Suddenly it dawned on them that being No. 1 in a business (again and again and again) often can lead to complacency and arrogance – much like Aesop's fable of *The Hare and the Tortoise* – whereas being second often can mean you're inclined to try harder.

As a result of this cunningly clever twist of thought, Green and Krone went on to launch Avis's legendary 'We Try Harder' campaign, which attracted many new customers to the car hire company they perceived as having their best interests at heart. Or, to be more specific: 'In just one year, the campaign literally changed the fortunes of the company. Prior to the campaign, Avis had just $34 million in revenue and losses of $3.2 million. One year later, revenues had jumped to $38 million and, for the first time in 13 years, Avis turned a profit of $1.2 million' (www.avis.com).

Ultimately, then, **Business Genius** is all about using our little grey cells (as Hercule Poirot would say) to add extra value (smarter thinking), and to work out smarter ways of working (smarter working) …

So, if you want to experience more **Genius** moments in the work that you do – whether it's finance in Frankfurt or sales in Shanghai, PR in Paris or HR in Houston (or social enterprise, marketing, IT, retail, training and development or whatever) – please remember it's not *what* you do that usually matters most, but *how* you go about doing it!

Or, to be more specific:

→ How we *see* (like Albert Moore with his OXO Tower).

→ How we *strategise* (like Abe Saperstein with his HGT).

→ How we *strive* (like Avis with its 'savvy' ad campaign).

As we're curiously about to explore …

'Be curious. A successful person is always going to be curious.'
Donald Trump ('Real Estate Titan' and author of *Think Like a Billionaire*)

HOW TO GET THE MOST OUT OF THIS BOOK

How you choose to read this book is entirely **UP!** to you:

→ If you want to read it from cover to cover, read it from cover to cover.

→ If you want to dip in and out, dip in and out.

→ If you want to zoom ahead to a specific section, please zoom ahead.

My only suggestion is that, if you really want to get the most out of this book, keep turning your **lines** of thought into **ladders** of thought …

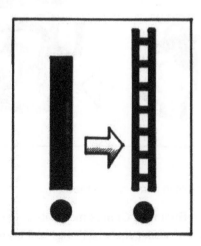

Why?

Because this is exactly what **Business Geniuses** do.

In direct contrast to **Non-Business Geniuses** – who often think along the lines of, 'It's just a sandwich!' or 'It's just a spring!' or 'It's just a sheep!' – **Business Geniuses** climb higher to see further. They look at the same sandwich, spring and sheep, and spot something more …

So please bear this in mind as you read on.

If you want more **Business Genius** moments in the work you do, it's not the lines of limitation that'll help you; it's the ladders of possibility.

And the best way to create these ladders is deceptively simple:

Question your assumptions

→ Ingvar Kamprad, for example, was the **Business Genius** entrepreneur who *questioned the assumption* that household furniture had to be pre-assembled and expensive. As a result, his Swedish flat-pack furniture company IKEA (which he named after his initials I. K.) elevated him to become 'the world's seventh richest man'!

→ Similarly, Louis Gerstner was the **Business Genius** executive who, during the 1990s, *questioned the assumption* that IBM was a broken machine, and beyond repair. As a result of his 'Who says elephants can't dance?' defiance, Gerstner managed to reverse the fortunes of the ailing giant, and once more steer them back into profit.

→ Or how about the story of the **Business Genius** secretary Bette Nesmith Graham? She was the **Genius** administrator from Texas who, in 1951, *questioned the assumption* that typed letters always needed to be retyped when little mistakes were made. Consequently, she went on to invent correction fluid, and her Liquid Paper Corporation eventually sold to Gillette in 1979 for $47.5 million.

There's plenty of evidence, therefore, to suggest that **Business Genius** is built upon **assumption-questioning**.

So here are a few more:

→ Jack Dorsey questioned the assumption that electronic communication needed to be longer than 140 characters, and went on to co-found the SMS for the internet: Twitter.

→ Kevin Costner – the Hollywood actor and film director – questioned the assumption that native Americans could only ever be portrayed as savages and villains in cowboy films, giving rise to the acclaimed *Dances With Wolves*, which won seven Academy Awards at the Oscars at the start of the 1990s.

Or here's a public sector example for you, if you'd welcome a **Business Genius** example that isn't only about profit, fame and fortune:

→ J. D. Millar – a Canadian engineer who worked for the Ontario Department of Transport in 1930 – questioned the assumption that unmarked roads (which were the norm back then) were a good idea, especially as so many cars were ending up in nasty head-on collisions. Millar simply suggested that the Department paint dotted white lines in the middle of the roads (to help separate the two-way traffic) and his inspired solution went on to save countless lives in countless countries!

So, the secret of getting the most out of this book is to keep reminding yourself that line thinking and ladder thinking are worlds apart:

A **line thinker**, for example, could easily read a book like this (i.e. a book on the psychology-side and creative-thinking side of business) and dismiss it as 'just common sense'!

Let's face it, they may be *right* (in the same way they're *right* about the sandwich, *right* about the spring and *right* about the sheep).

A **ladder thinker**, however, might see something more.

Goethe (the famous German poet and perceptive economic adviser to Duke Karl August of Weimar, back in 1906), for example, was an amazing ladder thinker who once wrote:

'Common sense is the genius of humanity'

Likewise, a line thinker could easily read a book like this (i.e. a book that's full of cartoons rather than complex corporate graphs and charts) and dismiss it as 'just childish'.

Again, they may be *right*. As I highlighted in my first book *Gen!us: Deceptively simple ways to become instantly smarter*, however, it could be argued that 'childish' and 'childlike' are *not* the same thing.

If I drew a picture of Iron Man, for example, and put it in a business book just for the fun of it, that would be 'childish'.

If, however, I use this same image to make a serious business point (i.e. how the world of business and the world of cartoons are more closely inter-connected than we might think) that would be 'childlike'.

Rather like this ...

Yup. Evidently, Stan Lee (the creator of Iron Man) based his character on Howard Hughes, the eccentric aviator and 'real' business billionaire.

Similarly, if I drew a picture of Charlie Brown and Snoopy and put it in a book on **Business Genius** (simply because I couldn't be bothered to write much text) that would definitely show strands of **Business Genius**, however, it'd also be rather 'childish', too.

But, what if I used the same image to demonstrate how targeted creative thinking can often hold the key to immense riches? Well, that would be 'childlike'. Rather like this …

Allegedly (according to www.celebritynetworth.com), the creative and **Business Genius** Charles M. Shultz left a lot more than 'peanuts' to his descendants when he died. Staggeringly, it's estimated that year-on-year his heirs receive more dollars from his doodles (in terms of royalties and merchandise) than the estates of John Lennon, Elizabeth Taylor and Jimi Hendrix combined.

Anyway, I hope you don't mind me mentioning it. I'm only doing so because I believe the childish/childlike distinction to be of such *high* importance.

In 1804, for example, line thinkers dismissed British inventor Richard Trevithick's 'iron horse' as little more than a childish fun ride, yet 20 years later it went on to become what we now know as the railways.

Similarly, in 1876, line thinkers at Western Union dismissed Alexander Graham Bell's 'idiotic' invention of a telephone as so childish it was 'hardly more than a toy'.

So let's ensure your brilliant **Business Genius** ideas don't get flattened in the same way.

Ladder thinking, as we've already mentioned, is what will help you to improve yourself, improve the way you get on with others, and improve what you achieve in business.

Here's one final thought, before we move on to the first chapter, '**UP!** your focus'.

If it wasn't for ladder thinking there'd be no skyscrapers (invented by William Le Baron Jenney – in Chicago, 1884 – when he came up with an improved way of building tall buildings using steel-girders); also there'd be no safety elevator either (invented by Elisha Otis in 1853, when he came up with an improved device to prevent elevators dropping through the air if a cable accidentally snapped); also there'd be no aviation industry!

This is because, since the time of Ancient Greece, people who wanted to fly like a bird naturally assumed the best way to do so was to look at birds, and copy the movement of their flapping wings.

What they failed to realise, however, was that, according to eagle expert Jemima Parry-Jones, we'd need to have 'chest muscles 2 m (6 ft) deep' to do the same thing, and we're simply not strong enough to copy them and flap 'wings down and backward like a rowing boat'.

Fortunately, however, along came the **Genius** thinker Sir George Cayley (1773–1857) who questioned this assumption, and ended up changing everything.

Cayley *stopped* looking at the movement of *birds*, and *started* looking at the movement of *kites*! As a result, according to author Rowland White in his book *The Big Book of Flight*: 'Cayley spotted what so many others had missed ... Perhaps flapping like a bird was not the best way to stay airborne.'

And, hopefully, from a **Business Genius** perspective, this 'flight nugget' helps to highlight what a *big difference* a simple idea can often make ...

'All achievement, all earned riches, have their beginning in an idea.'

Napoleon Hill (author of *Think and Grow Rich*)

PART 1
IMPROVE YOURSELF

'It is not the mountain we conquer but ourselves.'
Sir Edmund Hillary

UP! YOUR FOCUS

The first **B**lock and **L**imitation to **Business Genius** is **fruitless focus**.

Scattergun focus, for example, is often fruitless because there's no clear target.

(That's why Andrew Carnegie – the famous steel billionaire – once said 'a man should never scatter his shot'.)

Split focus, is often fruitless, too, because there are too many targets.

(That's why Tony Schwartz – the Harvard academic – highlights 'the magic of doing one thing at a time' and also having a 'not-to-do list'.)

Septic focus, however, is, perhaps, the most fruitless of all because it means we hit the target, but end up missing the point!

(That's why Sir Ken Robinson – the well-known creativity expert – stresses the importance of *not* viewing a situation 'in isolation of its context'.)

Take Kodak, for example. Why did it come close to collapse in 2012? Well, largely because of *septic focus*: it focused too much on the glories of its past (i.e. its 90 per cent market share in the 1970s) and not enough on the possibilities of the future (i.e. the rise of the digital camera).

Similarly, why was the telecoms industry simply out-smarted by the 'disruptive innovation' of Skype? Well, largely because telecoms firms focused too much on the *established competition*, and not enough on the *emerging competition*. As a result – according to business model authors Osterwalder and Pigneur – the 'free international calls' provider nobody took remotely seriously a few years back currently has over '400 million users, and generates in excess of $550 million revenue a year!'

So, please remember it's not usually *focus* itself that matters in business (because we're always focusing on something); it's fruitful focus that matters: focus that moves us closer towards our desired outcome (not further away from it).

And, talking about 'fruit', here's a thought ...

Back in the early 1800s the savvy Scotsman James Keiller didn't just concentrate on making quality 'orange spread'. Nope. There wouldn't have been much **Business Genius** in that.

By contrast, according to author Allan Burnett, he set his sights on a much juicier goal: 'Marketing Keiller's marmalade as a breakfast spread, rather than as a dessert, which was how marmalade had traditionally been consumed.'

As a result, Keiller's 'Marmalade for breakfast' focus helped turn him into a multi-millionaire.

Genius!

JAMES KEILLER
(1775-1839)

UP! YOUR FOCUS
NUGGET

Love him or loathe him, it's hard to deny that Simon Cowell (*The X Factor* impresario) has *surgical-strike focus* when it comes to business.

Let's face it, how else would the former EMI post boy – who spent 18 months 'pushing the trolley for £25 a week' – evolve into one of the world's highest-paid and most uber-influential media moguls?

Cowell's focus was amazingly simple from the start: he wanted to work in the music industry, and he wanted to reach the top! However, according to his biographer Tom Bower, when his request for a promotion at EMI was rejected (because he 'lacked any knowledge about music' at the time), he realised that his approach wasn't working. So what did he do? He changed tack, and promised himself – there and then – 'I'll work my way up.' And he achieved this by channelling 100 per cent of his efforts in one direction.

Talking of which, One Direction's success is a prime example of **Business Genius** focus in action.

Simon Cowell's usually too smart to stress about who's going to win *The X Factor*; he prefers to focus on who'll be the real winner after *The X Factor*. In an article by journalist Claire Beale entitled 'One Direction: a classic success story with a twist', for example, we learn how Simon (and his former chief marketer at Syco, Mark Hardy) were not that interested in creating another boy band, but they were very interested in creating a 'youth brand'.

Hardy went on to explain that, 'The best brands are built on listening and responding to what your audience wants,' so, during *The X Factor*, their primary focus was 'monitoring the social media profiles for all *The X Factor* contestants as early as two months before the final'. In other words, it wasn't necessarily the most 'votes' that mattered in their minds; it was the most 'buzz' (on Facebook and Twitter) that mattered. No wonder Cowell once said that, if you truly want to succeed in an industry as tough as the music industry, you need 'steel in your eyes!'

USEFUL TIPS AND ESCAPE STRATEGIES

So, if you genuinely want to **UP!** your focus – and achieve more **Genius** moments at work – here are three practical tips and strategies that can help:

1 FIND THE ONE

It can be easy sometimes, especially for creative types, to end up charging 'full steam ahead in all directions' (Al Ries, marketing professional and author). If you really want to make progress in business, however, it's often important to 'go small'.

That's why Gary Keller and Jay Papasan (authors of the best-seller *The ONE Thing: The surprisingly simple truth behind extraordinary results*) argue that 'extraordinary results are determined by how narrow you can make your focus', citing Google's focus on 'search' as a prime example. So, next time you're racing around like a headless chicken, why not take Keller and Papasan's advice and pinpoint what they call your 'lead domino'. Target that, and then – rather like this '/////////' – a chain reaction of multiple benefits flows from there. So, with this in mind, please answer their supreme **focus question**:

Q1 What's the one thing you could do today that by doing it everything else would become easier or unnecessary?

2 DON'T BOIL OCEANS

Top management consultancies often pride themselves on their ability to help businesses focus on what matters most. And one of the reasons they excel at this is because their focus is strategic.

Global management consulting firm McKinsey & Company, for example, recommends we 'Don't boil the ocean!' – because time is money, and we don't always need to know 'everything about everything' to progress. Far from it. What we *do* need to be able to *do* is 'distil' information effectively, rather than 'drown' in it.

That's why KPMG uses the strapline 'cutting through complexity', and placed those words on the side of a commuter catamaran on London's River Thames to help promote their consulting services (now that was **Business Genius**!).

Anyway, please consider this within the context of the work you do, because – as Sir Terry Leahy (the former CEO of Tesco) writes in his autobiography *Management in 10 Words* – often in business the solution is 'quite simple': Make things simple.

So, perhaps have a go at approaching this next focus question like Sherlock Holmes (who used to find the solutions to problems 'elementary'):

Q2 If you were to sum up your key workplace objectives using McKinsey's Rule of 3 (i.e. firstly, secondly, thirdly or A, B, C) what would those 3 elements be?

3 FLEX WHEN NECESSARY

Most business literature on focus is all about what psychologists call 'distraction control'.

In other words, it's about businesses working out precisely what they're about and where they're heading, and then making sure they go there without getting blown off course. Chris Zook of Bain & Company, for example, has written about this in his book, *Profit from the Core*.

Personally, I think it is sound advice, and I've often used a technique I call the **NEMO Technique,** which can help in this area.

The NEMO Technique simply means – in any given situation – you keep telling yourself '**N**othing **E**lse **M**atters' except for the **O**, which you then picture as an archery target! But let's leave that aside for now, because there's one other focal point we haven't mentioned yet: the dangers of over-focusing!

Like Captain Ahab (in *Moby Dick*) or, it could be argued, like the Tour de France cyclist Lance Armstrong who was so focused on winning (at any cost) he lost all sense of perspective, sometimes focusing too much can cause as many problems as focusing too little (as we'll explore in more detail later).

That's why focus experts like Tony Robbins and Paul McKenna don't just say, 'We always get more of what we focus on' or 'Whatever you consistently think about and focus upon, you move toward.' They also make clear how important it can be to 'change our approach' if something isn't working.

So, by all means 'hold the goal' in the work you do, but also make sure there's some wriggle room, too, in how you get there.

After all, many successful companies now work in a different sphere of business to when they started out: Virgin, for example, originally sold mail-order catalogues; Sony originally made rice-steamers; Nintendo made playing cards; and Nokia was in the wood pulp business.

Taking this into consideration, here's a third and final focus question for you:

Q3 Is the focus of your business still the best focus for your business, or does it need flexing?

Sadly, many organisations have ignored this question at their peril, and fallen into the trap of strategic drift (like Blockbuster UK and Clinton Cards). So, if you really want to travel the path of **Business Genius**, do your best to become 'bi-focal' (as American author and management expert Ken Blanchard advocates): 'Keep one eye on the present, and one eye on the future.'

By the way, if you really want to **UP!** your focus I'd also suggest you have a good chat with *highly focused people* you come across on your travels. Find out what works for them and then – using *exaptation* – explore innovative ways of applying these insights back to your own unique situation.

Here are two examples of my own, which may be of interest:

1 JON CALLARD (KICKER FOR THE ENGLAND RUGBY TEAM)

Someone I know called Jon Callard (who was the kicker for the England rugby team: 1993–1997) told me that different kickers would invariably use their own preferred focus technique.

One, for example, would focus on the line of his kick; another would focus on a head in the crowd and aim for that.

The secret of Jon's focus, however, wasn't sight but sound.

In a stadium full of many thousands of people, he found that sound was the ultimate distraction, so he'd focus on a different sound to blank it out. 'When I was kicking,' he said, 'there was only the ball, the posts, and me. Nothing else. My primary focus was the sound of my foot hitting the ball and listening to whether it made a "pop" sound (which I wanted) or a "slap" sound (which I didn't).'

So, here's a thought for you. If you were the **Business Genius** you aspire to be, what might that sound like? What specific words might others use to sum up your amazing business results? What key business messages would you most want others to hear?

2 HUGH GRIFFITHS (FORMER RAF TORNADO FAST-JET AVIATOR AND TACTICS INSTRUCTOR)

Someone else I know, Hugh Griffiths (who used to fly Tornado Jets for the RAF and now runs Inzpire, a business-performance consultancy), suggested another highly effective way for sharpening focus: 'In an emergency it's critical to focus on what's truly important!'

'In Hollywood movies, for example,' Hugh explained, 'when a plane's in trouble, you see pilots flicking all kinds of switches and screaming out "Mayday, Mayday", and usually yelling some instructions to the person next to them. What happens in reality, however, is very very simple. You keep telling yourself to fly the plane.'

Yes, it might sound unbelievably obvious, but, as Hugh explained, there have been examples of pilots who have been so busy focusing on the emergency, they've forgotten to 'fly the plane', and the plane's accidentally stalled at 38,000 feet!

Within the context of your own **Business Genius** focus, you may want to apply a similar strategy.

Of course the work you do isn't literally going to be the same as flying at speed at 200 feet off the ground with an engine on fire (or, at least, let's hope not) but the underlying principle is equally relevant. Or, as Hugh puts it: 'The principle of "fly the plane" is very relevant in business. All too often organisations focus on profit or sales, but cashflow can be critical. You need oil in the engine to keep in the air!'

So, once again, focus and keeping things simple appear to be inter-connected, especially when the pressure's on. This is why, in an emergency context, RAF pilots are trained to 'aviate, navigate, and then communicate' (in other words, 'Keep the plane flying, then point it in a safe direction, and then tell others what's going on'). Who knows? If this powerful simplicity works for them, it may well work for you ...

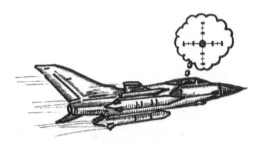

BUSINESS GENIUS IN ACTION: NEXT STEPS ...

In summary, if you want to **UP!** your focus, here's how:

❶ Pinpoint what fruitful focus and fruitless focus mean to *you* (to help you focus on what matters most).

❷ Investigate how your current tasks link up to the bigger picture (to avoid the trap of 'septic focus').

❸ **L**everage the power of NEMO, **N**othing **E**lse **M**atters (to strengthen your 'distraction control').

❹ **O**rchestrate a plan for focusing that fits your personal preferences (to make it easier for you to leverage the power of sight or sound, so you can stay on course).

❺ **T**arget the one thing in your day that will have the greatest impact (to create a positive domino effect on everything else).

And, above all else, remember to 'Fly the plane!'.

UP!SPIRATION
'Concentration is the key to economic results.'
Peter Drucker (writer, professor and management consultant)

UP! YOUR CONFIDENCE

The second **B**lock and **L**imitation to **Business Genius** is a
lack of confidence.

The good news, however, is that, if this resonates with you,
you're in good company. Many **Business Geniuses** – from
Frank W. Woolworth to Thomas Edison – started out with low
levels of confidence, yet managed to **UP!** their confidence as
their careers evolved.

Anyway, what we need to remember is that no one is 100 per
cent confident all the time. We have, instead, what are called
'pockets of confidence'.

A pilot, for example, might feel highly confident landing a plane
in a storm (because they've experienced doing so many times
before) yet feel like a quivering wreck if they had to perform in
a West End show (on the opening night of a play they'd never
rehearsed for). In fact, even the acting **Genius** Lawrence Olivier
never really lost his stage fright, but let's not go there …

The point is, next time you lack confidence, please be kind on
yourself, and bear in mind that confidence (which comes from
the Latin word *confidere*) means trust – i.e. 'Trust in our natural
ability to do something' – and luckily this trust can be developed
and nurtured.

To achieve this, though, it can help to be aware of what Martin
Perry calls the 'Confidence Spectrum' (which he explores in
detail in his book *Confidence Booster Workout: 10 steps to
beating self-doubt*). Put simply, Perry's Confidence Spectrum
stretches along five zones:

Arrogance; supreme confidence; confidence;
self-doubt; low self-esteem

As you can see, confidence is in the middle, whilst arrogance and low self-esteem are at either end. But here's the intriguing *mind twist*.

Over the years, I've asked all kinds of seminar groups the following question: 'What's the key difference between confidence and arrogance? Where does one become the other?' And many have struggled to locate a precise point. Perry, however, sums this up brilliantly with one word: *assumptions*.

Why?

Well, Perry uses the metaphor of someone running a race. A *confident* runner, for example, would say, 'I can win' (i.e. natural ability + trust).

A *supremely confident* runner, meanwhile, would say, 'I will win', because it's basically the same with a touch of belief thrown in.

But here's the difference! An *arrogant* person says, 'I always win.'

Can you hear the difference?

Admittedly, they may well win and, statistically, they may even be 99.9 per cent likely to win. If they *assume* they'll win, however, that would be arrogant!

So, no wonder arrogance is ubiquitous in the world of business: *arrogant* bosses who *assume* their opinion is the only one worth listening to; *arrogant* managers who *assume* they don't need to listen to what's being said because they know it all already. You know what I mean …

'And what about the other end of the spectrum?' you may well ask.

Well, if a person's self-trust gets damaged – perhaps because they've given a poor business presentation, having fumbled their lines, or perhaps let their team down on a project and lost a crucial deal – that's when confidence can often spiral down into one of two things:

→ *Self-doubt* (i.e. natural ability – trust), in which a runner might say, 'I'll probably lose'; or

→ *Low self-esteem*, where a lack of self-worth triggers an equally harmful assumption: 'I always lose, so what's the point in even running?'

'Fair enough,' you may well be thinking. 'So what? I can think of plenty of **Business Geniuses** who've been incredibly arrogant, and it hasn't done them any harm. And I can also think of many **Business Geniuses** who, deep down, have low self-esteem, yet have still managed to prosper.'

I agree.

All I'm saying here is that if you really want to *maximise* your **Business Genius**, confidence (rather than *arrogance* or low *self-esteem*) is more likely to help you. Or, as academics would say, *self-efficacy* is most likely to help you, which is a term Professor Bandura of Stanford came up with, and means 'our belief in our ability to succeed in specific situations'.

Consider David Seidler, for example. When he was a young boy he suffered from a nervous stutter (which undermined his confidence, and made his stutter even worse). 'Don't worry,' his parents would say, 'even Bertie [King George VI of England] had a stutter.' Seidler could easily have dismissed this insight and become increasingly withdrawn, but he didn't. Years later, as **Business Geniuses** often do, he ingeniously transformed what could be considered his disadvantage into an advantage and ended up writing a screenplay on stuttering called *The King's Speech*, which was crowned best film at the Oscars in 2011!

UP! YOUR CONFIDENCE
NUGGET

The actor Sean Connery – who many still regard as the ultimate James Bond – was once asked about the secret of his success. His answer was simple: 'Confidence, confidence, confidence.'

Now, let's face it, that was probably easy for him to say this (with his movie-star good looks and muscle-man physique) but the point Connery was making was an important one. Often, in business, as Peter Jones – the author of *Tycoon* and UK entrepreneur and *Dragon's Den* investor – writes:

> **'The bottom line is, if you don't believe in yourself or your idea, why should anyone else?'**

And Connery is living proof of this.

When he turned up for the Bond audition in 1962, he was aware he had only an outside chance of winning the role, so he decided to 'put on a bit of an act'.

He strolled into the room with the power and grace of a cat (having been trained by the Swedish movement and posture specialist Yat Malmgren) and did everything he could to ooze self-assuredness and impress film producers Cubby Broccoli and Harry Saltzman. And it paid off.

According to Connery's biographer Christopher Bray, the moment he left the audition, they knew they'd got their man: 'It was the sheer self-confidence he exuded,' Broccoli went on to say. Please note, however, for confidence to work effectively, *you* need to believe it first (intra-psychically) otherwise – as neuro-linguistic programming research indicates – there's a danger your body language and physiology will soon give the game away, regardless of the words we use. So, remember, confidence matters: 'Not so fast, Goldfinger ...'

**USEFUL TIPS AND
ESCAPE STRATEGIES**

Unfortunately, there's no magic wand that's guaranteed to instantly **UP!** your confidence. Here are three tips and strategies, however, which can significantly help you to help yourself:

1 EXPAND YOUR PRESENCE

Many confidence experts argue that charisma is something you're either born with, or you're not. So let's forget about charisma. Let's focus instead on presence, because presence is something we *can* do something about!

According to presence expert Meribeth Bunch in her book *Creating Confidence: How to develop your personal power and presence*, 'Presence has to do with a sense of space and how to use it.'

With this in mind, here are *two* practical ways to expand our presence.

Firstly, Bunch explains, we need to keep telling ourselves, 'I want to be here.' Yes, I know it sounds a bit bizarre, but think about it. What usually happens when we're lacking in confidence? We tell ourselves the complete opposite. For example, ever seen someone give a talk and then move on to the Q & A part? Most have vanished before the first question …

Secondly, linked to the above, Bunch recommends that – wherever we are – we imagine we're back in the comfort of our own home. Why? 'Because our behaviour changes when we feel at home'. It's our turf, so to speak; it's where we usually have the upper hand, and psychological advantage. So, if you want to **UP!** your presence consider this:

Q1 How much personal space (energy field) are you occupying at the moment, and how much more confident would you feel if it was 10 times larger or 100 times larger?

2 HARMONISE YOUR MESSAGE

Over the years I've worked with all kinds of people in companies helping them to improve their presentation skills. Intriguingly, one of the things they find most challenging is knowing what to do with their hands when speaking to an audience.

Keep your hands behind your back and risk looking too formal; keep your hands in your pockets and risk looking too casual; keep moving your hands all over the place (and nervously fiddle with a pen, or shuffle your papers) and you risk deeply irritating your audience.

Well, evidently, the secret is that it doesn't really matter what you do with hands, as long as you use them 'in harmony with your message'. So, if you want to emphasise *one* point, maybe raise *one* finger and say, 'If there's *one* thing you take away from this presentation, I hope it's this'; or, if you want to say, 'The whole department needs to come together on this,' bring your hands together. It's called the 'the puppetry of the hands', so next time you watch a confident speaker, simply watch and learn how they do it.

3 KEEP FORGETTING YOURSELF

Many people who lack confidence in business do so because they're incredibly self-conscious.

They become prisoners of the four enemies of confidence, which Perry identifies as:

❶ worrying too much what others think;

❷ doubting our skills and abilities;

❸ continually comparing ourselves with others;

❹ fearing failure.

The best antidote to this is simply to do the opposite.

For example, one of the best bits of advice I ever came across – from a presentation skills perspective – was to think of ourselves as a messenger. You're simply there to hand over a message, and what others do with that message is a different story. In other words 'It's not about you!'

And the moment this happens our presentations normally improve because the best presentations – according to

Professor of Psychology Adrian Furnham – are usually less about presentation skills, and more about anxiety management.

Finally, here's some food for thought to bring it back to the world of **Business Genius**. Hermes, in Ancient Greek mythology, was not only the messenger of Zeus (with his snazzy winged boots), he was also the God of commerce and merchants. Furthermore, if it wasn't for the Ancient Greeks we wouldn't have companies called Nike, Argos, Omega or Amazon at all …

BUSINESS GENIUS IN ACTION: NEXT STEPS …

In summary, if you want to **UP!** your confidence, here's how:

❶ **P**inpoint where you see yourself on the 'Confidence Spectrum' (so you can start questioning the assumptions that can hold you back).

❷ **I**nvestigate the confidence success stories of others (because – as we explored in the David Seidler example – finding out how others have managed to turn their setbacks into stepping stones can often inspire us to get beyond whatever's standing in our way).

❸ **L**everage the power of self-belief, as Sean Connery did (for if you don't believe in yourself or your idea, why should anyone else?).

❹ **O**rchestrate a plan for telling yourself, 'I want to be here' (to enable you to expand your personal presence).

❺ **T**arget the four enemies of confidence to silence your inner critic (because the less you worry about what others think, doubt your own abilities, continually compare yourself with others, and fear failure, there's a high probability your confidence level will instantly increase).

UP!SPIRATION
'Confidence attracts.'
Deborah Meaden (UK entrepreneur and *Dragon's Den* investor)

UP! YOUR RESILIENCE

The third major **Block** and **Limitation** to **Business Genius** is **limited resilience**.

Or, to put it another way, not being able to bounce back from setbacks, which is an amazingly important skill if we want to excel at work!

The young César Ritz, for example, could easily have quit the hotel industry after he was fired as a wine waiter and told, 'You're an unsuitable candidate for the hotel trade!' But Ritz wasn't prepared to let this happen.

Similarly, Walt Disney – who once got fired by a newspaper editor because 'he lacked imagination and had no good ideas' – could easily have taken this crushing criticism to heart (and opted for a less creative career path instead) but he, too, was too driven to let his ambitions get thwarted.

Or how about the actor Ben Affleck, whose career struck an all-time low in 2005 when the movie *Surviving Christmas* came out. He must have been tempted to pack it in, as they say, but as Nassim Nicholas Taleb (the author of *Black Swan* and *Anti-Fragile*) highlights, 'Tough times don't last, tough people do.'

According to Affleck's *Bourne Identity* best friend Matt Damon (in a *ShortList* magazine interview, August 2013) Affleck's agent said to him: 'OK, this [the movie] is going to come out and it's going to be really bad. This is it. This is the bottom of the mountain right here, we start walking uphill today.'

Consequently, Affleck found the inner strength to pick himself up and dust himself off and, step-by-step, he went on to not only act in, but also direct, *Argo* – a movie about an ingenious science-fiction plan to rescue hostages, which catapulted his career to an all-time high!

So please bear this in mind within the context of the work you do.

Few **Business Geniuses** enjoy careers where everything runs smoothly from start to finish. On the contrary. Just look at the careers of everyone – from Milton Hershey to Henry Ford and even H. J. Heinz – who took the knocks, and yet still found a way to clamber back from bankruptcy.

In fact, it could be argued that some industries – like the music industry and the world of book-writing – would barely exist at all if it wasn't for resilient people doggedly carrying on in the face of constant rejection and setbacks.

In the early days, for example, the guitarist Mark Knopfler had very little money. So did he let that hold him back? No. He just named his band Dire Straits. Years later, when he was making significant amounts of money, envious delivery men made the flippant remark that he was simply getting 'money for nothing'. So did he let that stinging comment dent his pride? No. He just used it as the title for his next song, and ended up making even more money!

Similarly, it's said that J. K. Rowling's *Harry Potter* was rejected by 12 publishers before it finally got signed up by Bloomsbury and, even then – according to www.literaryrejections.com – she was told by her editor to 'get a day job because there's little chance of making money in children's books.' There are even instances when despondent authors have thrown their scripts into the bin out of despair, only to have them retrieved by partners who've helped to bolster their resilience. Stephen King, for example, did this with *Carrie* (after it had been rejected by 30 publishers), but then later went on to sell over 350 million books!

So, if it's **Business Genius** you're after, please be aware that, even if you fall down, you don't always have to stay down. For, as Joe Simpson (the mountaineer of *Touching the Void* fame, who literally fell off a mountain in The Andes because his colleague had to cut the rope before they both fell off) survived to say: 'Success is choice, not chance.'

GENIUS

UP! YOUR RESILIENCE
NUGGET

A classic example of **Business Genius** resilience is the Honda story Tony Robbins used to give as part of his 'Awaken the Giant Within' seminars.

Robbins highlighted how Soichiro Honda's commercial ambitions were thwarted time and time again. However, he refused to give up. Literally.

To begin with, in 1938, the specialised piston rings he strived to create were rejected by Toyota because they weren't of a sufficiently high standard.

So, did he call it a day? No. He went back to college to improve them, only to have his 'absurd designs' mocked by peers and teachers alike.

Then, two years later, he finally secured a contract with Toyota only to face a new problem. Japan was 'gearing up for war' and there was no concrete available to help him build his factory. So he got creative, and made his own concrete.

Anyway. During the war his factory was bombed, not just once but twice!

And it didn't stop there.

Because Japan had a severe shortage of raw materials, the enterprising Honda encouraged his team to go off and 'pick up extra gasoline cans' dropped by the Americans as 'gifts from President Truman'. But then an earthquake levelled his premises. Was that it? No.

After the war, because 'there was a gasoline shortage' Honda decided to attach a small motor to his bicycle to help him get around. Other people loved his invention, but he lacked the capital needed to produce them. So what did he do? He wrote '18,000 personal letters' to bike shops across Japan asking for assistance, managing to persuade 5,000 to invest. And, even then, his new bikes were considered too bulky, so he had to design a smaller one called the Supercub. Anyway, the reason for saying all this is because Honda's 'Power of Dreams' organisation (which now employs over 100,000 people) wouldn't exist if it hadn't have been for Honda's resilience, so no wonder he once said: 'Success is 99 per cent failure.'

If you want to **UP!** your resilience, here are three practical tools that can help add value to that process:

1 EMBRACE LEARNED OPTIMISM

According to research by positive psychology experts Martin Seligman and Ilona Boniwell, the key difference between **optimists** and **pessimists** is linked to how they process information.

Imagine a good event has just happened in a business, for example, such as winning a brand new contract.

An optimist would probably process this information as follows:

→ In an *internal* way, e.g. 'I helped win this contract'.

→ In a *stable* way, e.g. 'I sense I may have a talent for winning contracts'.

→ In a *global* way, e.g. 'If I helped win this one, there's a good chance I could help us win more'.

A pessimist, however, is likely to do the complete opposite. They're likely to interpret the same event as follows:

→ In an *external* way, e.g. 'They must have been desperate to choose us!'.

→ In an *unstable* way, e.g. 'Sure, I helped win it, but I just got lucky'.

→ In a *specific* way, e.g. 'This was a one-off. We're bound to lose the rest'.

Intriguingly, however, if they had *not* won that contract, the reverse would have happened.

An optimist probably would have processed this 'bad event' as follows:

→ In an *external* way, e.g. 'Maybe they wanted a less innovative supplier'.

→ In an *unstable* way, e.g. 'Never mind. This now frees me up to focus on securing more lucrative contracts'.

→ In a *specific* way, e.g. 'OK, this specific situation didn't work out, but that happens sometimes. There are plenty of other commercial opportunities out there worth pursuing'.

A pessimist, meanwhile, would think:

→ In an *internal* way, e.g. 'The whole thing's my fault. That's why we lost it'.

→ In a *stable* way, e.g. 'Here we go again. I'll never win a contract!'.

→ In a *global* way, e.g. 'Seems like we lose every contract we try to go for'.

Please bear this in mind with your own resilience. How you choose to interpret events – both good and bad – can either be your best friend who spurs you on, or your worst enemy who drags you back.

2 BECOME THAT DIAMOND

Diamonds are the toughest natural element on earth. According to author Barry Farber in his book *Diamonds Under Pressure: Five steps to turning adversity into success*, however, the only reason they're so strong is because they've spent millions of years buried underground having their carbon crystals pressed in on from all sides, before being exploded up to the surface by volcanic activity.

So you may want to bear this in mind, if and when you feel crushed by your workplace experiences. They may be dreadful. However, if you can *reframe* your situation in an empowering way, you're more likely to be able to bounce back from it.

Oh, and if you're not too keen on the diamond metaphor, feel free to choose another one. Farber, for example, also points out how resilience is like the wings of a butterfly, saying: 'In order to escape its cocoon, the butterfly must band its wings against the sides again and again, which gives its wings the strength to fly.'

3 'STAND UP EIGHT'

There's an old Japanese proverb that states, 'Fall down seven times, stand up eight' and, in many ways, this sums up resilience.

Resilience means having that dogged determination to keep going no matter what, rather like the tiny spider in the Robert the Bruce story.

So next time you're tempted to give up – and it's bound to happen once in a while – remind yourself that **Business Genius** and 'the spirit of enterprise' are closely connected, and 'the spirit of enterprise' is all about an ongoing process of 'do-learn-do'.

In summary, if you want to **UP!** your resilience, here's how:

1 **P**inpoint the reality that few careers run smoothly from start to finish (to help you develop a more balanced perspective with your own work).

2 **I**nvestigate how others have managed to spring back from setbacks (because – as we saw with Ritz, Disney, Affleck and Honda – sometimes the seemingly impossible can become possible, if we use *flexible persistence*).

3 **L**everage the power of positive psychology and learned optimism (to ensure you prosper, both now and in the future).

4 **O**rchestrate a plan for turning your adversity into success (for with a little imaginative thinking – as we saw with Mark Knopfler – there's virtually always a way of spinning a perceived disadvantage into a perceived advantage).

5 **T**arget the learning experience inside every error of judgement (simply because we can often learn more from our mistakes – or 'crucible moments' as they're sometimes called – than our business triumphs).

UP!SPIRATION
'True success is about hanging on when everyone else lets go.'
Karren Brady (vice-chairman of West Ham United and one of the UK's leading business figures)

UP! YOUR STRESS MANAGEMENT SKILLS

T he fourth **B**lock and **L**imitation to **Business Genius** is
ineffective stress management.

This doesn't mean ineffective in an unkind way. Far from it. It simply means that effective stress management is more vital than it's ever been, and the reason for this can be summed up in one word:

Spillage

Take air traffic control, for example.

Years ago I met someone who worked for air traffic control, which I'd always assumed to be an amazingly stressful profession.

'It isn't really,' I was told, much to my surprise. 'When you're *at work*, stress levels frequently run high (because you're helping to avoid collisions and land planes safely), but the moment you've *left work*, the stress stops. It's not your problem any more, it's someone else's!'

In the world of air traffic control, you're either *at work*, or you've *left work*, so 'spillage' isn't that much of an issue.

Few other jobs, however, share such clear-cut boundaries.

How many of us, for example, often take work home with us to do in the evenings, or at weekends? How many of us have a nervous *tweet*ch, and are continually checking our business emails, or surfing the net because of FOMO (fear of missing out)? How many of us enjoy the freedom to escape work entirely without a call from our boss, or a client, saying 'I know you're on holiday, but …'?

The point we're making here is that the modern business world (which is obviously 24/7 and globally connected) is fantastic in so many ways, but it's deeply flawed when it comes to 'spillage' and stress.

This is simply because our bodies haven't evolved fast enough to deal with the modern stresses of the modern age (or the 'Attention Economy'– as authors Davenport and Beck like to call it – where we're continually under pressure to pay attention to an infinite variety of different people and things).

Millions of years ago, for example, if we were being chased by a sabre-toothed tiger, our bodies would naturally release adrenaline (to help us run away), or nor-adrenaline (to help us stand and fight). Either way, these life-preserving chemicals would get used up in the process of handling that specific threat. Nowadays, however, these same chemicals get pumped into our bloodstream (to help us tackle multiple workplace threats and challenges) but they don't always get used up, and they don't always stop coming!

They just bubble up inside as we sit at our desk, or huff and puff in our office meetings, and brace ourselves for yet another tiger to pounce.

From a **Business Genius** perspective, therefore, it's essential we learn how to **flick off the switch** (from time to time) or the chances are we'll end up doing ourselves more harm than good.

Besides, we only need to look at Professor Stephen Palmer and Lynda Strickland's book, *Stress Management*, to see the long list of psychological, physiological and physical effects stress has the power to trigger. And we're not just talking about sweaty palms, breathlessness and 98 per cent of all headaches here.

Too much stress can also lead to everything from nightmares to backache, being cynical to being jealous, and sometimes even poor time management to withdrawing from supportive relationships.

In fact, in Japan they even have a phenomenon called *karoshi* (death through overwork), so no wonder Professor Cary Cooper calls stress 'the disease of our time'.

If we really want to flick off the switch to excel, however, we need to be able to flick our thinking first.

For example, we need to be aware that stress (i.e. the imbalance between the *perceived demands* placed upon us, and the *perceived resources* we have to handle them) ultimately means **psychological self-strangulation**.

Yes, I know this is a horrible phrase – so please forgive me for using it – but if you go back to the Roman and Anglo-Saxon origin of most of the words used in the English language to describe stress, it's not too hard to spot the link:

> *Stringere* (stress) = to squeeze/draw tight
> *Angere* (anxiety) = to choke
> *Tendere* (tension) = to stretch
> *Wyrgan* (worry) = to strangle

So, if you really want to **UP!** your **Business Genius** stress management, please remember the thoughts we think can either wind us up (and squeeze us into a tight little ball) or help us to unwind …

UP! YOUR STRESS MANAGEMENT NUGGET

Few industries have prospered more from the world of stress than the tourism industry.

After all, why else do so many people – year-on-year – spend vast sums of money lounging by hotel pools, or travelling up snowy mountains to spa retreats, if it's not to chill out and unwind?

Well, it could be argued that the **Business Genius** who set this in motion was the Victorian entrepreneur Thomas Cook.

Back in 1841 Cook – who was an ex-preacher and part of the Temperance Movement (which disapproved of alcohol and its impact on social well-being) – decided to commission a special train to take his Temperance group members from Leicester to Loughborough to hear a talk, and for this arrangement he decided to charge them 'one shilling a head' (source: www.thomascook.com).

At the time this was a highly innovative idea because, up until then, people had usually arranged, and paid for, their own travel arrangements.

Cook, however, was very smart because he found a way of taking the hassle and stress out of travel for other people. All they needed to do was buy a single ticket from him, and he'd sort out the rest. And it all grew from there …

In 1845 he started to make the whole process more commercial (even providing a 'handbook for the journey' which was 'the forerunner of the modern holiday brochure'). By 1855 he was taking tourists to mainline Europe. In the 1870s he came up with yet more **Business Genius** ideas such as 'hotel coupons' and his 'circular note' (which was a 'forerunner of the traveller's cheque'). In 1869, he arranged his first trip up the Nile, and thereafter he started to take travellers on relaxing journeys around the world.

THOMAS COOK
(1808 ~ 1892)

USEFUL TIPS AND ESCAPE STRATEGIES

If you want to **UP!** the quality of your stress management skills, here are three practical tips and strategies that can help:

1 CHANGE YOUR SELF-TALK

Cognitive behavioural therapy (CBT) – which has become incredibly popular in recent years for supporting individuals suffering from work-related stress – is built upon a simple idea: *Change how you think* and you can often *Change how you feel.*

Supposing something goes wrong at work, for example, and you beat yourself up about it: 'Everything's my fault!' you sigh with your head in your hands, 'I'll lose my job, and I'll never get another one in this challenging business climate etc.'

Of course this may well be the case (so my apologies if it is).

What CBT would suggest, however, is that thinking this way is only likely to escalate your stress levels, rather than diminish them. Far better to imagine you're like a scientist in a white coat looking at the evidence of what you're saying under the microscope, both coolly and objectively.

For example, you may find it useful to draw a circle that represents 100 per cent, and then ask yourself, 'Is 100 per cent of this problem 100 per cent my fault?' More often than not, you'll probably find that much of it still is, but probably *not* all of it. And, when you start to realise that 20 per cent is, perhaps, your team's fault, and 15 per cent is, perhaps, your manager's fault, and 5 per cent was owing to unforeseen circumstances, suddenly your stress levels will lower, as that 100 per cent becomes 60 per cent. This isn't to say that shifting the blame onto others is the key; it's simply to say that challenging our thinking errors (such as magnifying what went wrong, or minimising what went right) can be a highly effective way of reframing a stressful situation.

With this in mind, next time you feel stressed at work, you may want to ask yourself this question:

Q1 What am I telling myself to feel this way (and how much better might I feel if I told myself something different)?

2 REMEMBER TO BREATHE

Evidence suggests that, when we feel under pressure, our breathing automatically changes; it starts to become more rapid, and it starts to become more shallow.

That's why everyone, from martial artists to Hollywood stunt professionals, knows the importance of *deliberately* breathing more slowly, and more deeply, to reverse this process, and bring their breathing back into alignment once again.

(Clearly, if you're someone who suffers from panic attacks or breathing problems of any kind, please seek professional medical help as your first port of call.)

For what it's worth, however, over the years I've personally found all kinds of Eastern exercises – from Tai Chi to yoga – can make a big difference to workplace stress, as can Western techniques ranging from autogenic exercises (when you keep telling yourself 'My breathing is relaxed and effortless') to Harvard Professor Dr Herbert Benson's technique (where you keep repeating the mantra 'One' to yourself, to help clear your head of all other thoughts).

Finally, I was once told we can't breathe *in* until we've breathed *out*, and so I found (counter-intuitively) that only by breathing out for 10 seconds, would my lungs naturally refill.

Q2 It's sometimes said that 'When you control your breathing, you control your life.' What difference might *improved breathing* potentially make to yours?

3 E + R = O

There's nothing particularly new about this E + R = O equation, but that doesn't stop many still finding its wisdom highly valuable.

Put simply, it stands for **Event + Response = Outcome** and it shows how, although we can't always change the *events* in our lives, we can often change our *response* to them and this, in turn, can often influence the overall *outcome*.

In Switzerland in 1541, for example, an *event* happened that put the Swiss goldsmiths and jewellers of Geneva under considerable stress.

A new law was introduced – by the Protestant reformer Jean Calvin – which banned the wearing of jewellery. This was totally out of their control, and there was nothing they could do to change it.

What they could do, however, was change their *response* to this *event*, and that's precisely what they did. They decided to use a bit of **Business Genius** to get around the ban, and they became watchmakers instead!

By 1601 they'd created the first ever Watchmakers Guild in the world and, as for the overall *outcome*? Well, why else would we have companies today ranging from Rolex to Patek Philippe, and Omega to TAG Heuer, in existence (contributing more than $22 billion to the Swiss economy each year)?

In summary, if you want to **UP!** your stress management skills, here's how:

1 **P**inpoint specific times when you can flick off the switch (because, unless you create a bit of me-time or being-time for yourself – in the manic 24/7 'Attention Economy' we live in – nobody else will, and your personal batteries will soon run flat).

2 **I**nvestigate which symptoms of stress could apply to you (for improved self-awareness is often the first step towards improved well-being).

3 **L**everage the power of self-talk (to help you change your state because – as CBT and other branches of psychology highlight – *how* we think can either wind us up or help us to unwind).

4 **O**rchestrate a plan for improving your breathing (by doing yoga, Tai Chi, meditation, or whatever, but please go easy with this one, for obvious medical reasons).

5 **T**arget what you *can* do something about; not what you *can't* (because, as the principle of E + R = O illuminates, although we can't always control the events in our lives, we can often control our responses to those events, and that, in turn, inevitably will have an impact on the final outcome!).

UP!SPIRATION

'The greatest weapon against stress is our ability to choose one thought over another.'

William James (American philosopher and psychologist)

UP! YOUR TIME MANAGEMENT SKILLS

The fifth **B**lock and **L**imitation to **Business Genius** is
unproductive time management.

The reasons for this are many and varied. However, here are the
top two:

❶ We mistakenly think we can do everything.

(We can't.)

❷ We mistakenly think that time management is all about time.

(It isn't.)

Time management is really about *psychology*.

It's about our personal values (*what's most important to us*),
procrastination (*our desire to put off the pain*), and a rich
tapestry of other psychological threads, too, from being over-
fussy (*perfectionism*) to hopelessly dreamy (*lacking in focus*).

If we want to **UP!** our time management skills, we need to
acknowledge there's usually more to it than just asking for more
concise reports, having stand-up meetings, or using the 4Ds
(i.e. do now, do later, drop, delegate).

Ever noticed, for example, how some people always seem to do
too much and always end up feeling overwhelmed?

Or how others *almost* succeed, and *almost* finish what they
start, yet keep switching direction at the last minute instead of
completing?

Well, according to Dr Eric Berne – who developed a style of
psychotherapy known as Transactional Analysis back in the
1960s – this might not be entirely coincidental.

It could be because they have an *always script*, or an *almost
script*.

Here's why.

Berne was curious why people kept doing things that seemed so blatantly against their self-interest. Why, for example, might someone lurch from one stressful job straight into another stressful job? It didn't make sense. But then it started to make sense from a 'script' point of view.

Berne suggested that from the moment we're born – to the age of about seven – we create a 'pattern', which helps us to make sense of ourselves, others and the world we live in. These patterns are what he calls 'Life Scripts', and we all have them!

Fortunately, however, because life is decisional, with sufficient self-awareness we have the power to change our script and write a better one.

Without this self-awareness, however, we can easily get locked into repeating the same old familiar pattern. Next time you tut to yourself, for example, you've probably gone into script, because *tut* = *typical*, and *typical* = *been here before*.

The reason I'm saying all this is because, on the face of it, it's easy to *assume* that the person who feels overwhelmed – from a time management perspective – is overwhelmed because they're doing too much. In script theory, however, it may be the opposite: perhaps the person is doing too much in order to feel overwhelmed, yet again.

Enough theory, though. Let's move on to the practicals.

The key to productive time management is to remember psychologist Michael Altshuler's mantra: 'The bad news is time flies. The good news is you're the pilot.'

That's to say, what matters most with time is *how* we *choose* to spend the 86,400 seconds we have available in every day, and the 168 hours we have available in every week and, basically, we have four choices:

❶ *Emergency* time = immediate value.

❷ *Enrichment* time = residual value.

❸ *Entrapment* time = superficial value.

❹ *Empty* time = no value.

As you can see, it doesn't take a **Genius** to work out where **Business Geniuses** usually choose to spend most of their time.

Of course there'll be urgent deadlines that they need to meet from time to time (emergencies), and meetings they get drawn into attending, which turn out to be pointless (entrapments), but the bottom line is that **Business Geniuses** are very good at being the *pilots* of their own time.

Bill Gates, for example, could easily have loafed on the sofa aimlessly watching TV for much of his youth (empty time). By contrast, however, he chose to build up his business (enrichment time) and didn't take a single day off for the whole of his 20s!

Now I'm not suggesting you go this far. On the contrary. Enrichment time can also mean spending quality time with your loved ones, or giving yourself a well-earned break (what Covey called 'recreation'). All I'm saying is that **Business Geniuses** know busy-ness is not the same as business, and activity is not the same as achievement. What matters most is productive time management, and prioritising those non-urgent enriching activities that yield the greatest ROI ...

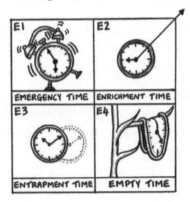

UP! YOUR TIME MANAGEMENT SKILLS NUGGET

Arguably the most successful time management **Business Genius** ever was Stephen Covey (the author of *The 7 Habits of Highly Effective People* and *First Things First*).

Before Covey's ground-breaking ideas were published in 1989 there weren't very many books on time management, and of the few in existence they all seemed obsessed with *the clock*. When Covey and his colleagues arrived on the scene, however, they offered a very different approach: *the compass*. In a nutshell, what this meant was this:

During Covey's effectiveness seminars, he'd put a large transparent vase on a table and then fill it with rocks. 'Is it full?' he'd say, and the audience would usually say 'Yes!'.

Then he'd reach under the table and bring out some pebbles and pour them into the same vase. 'Is it full now?' he'd say. Once again he'd get a 'Yes!'. But then he'd end up pouring in some sand, and finally water ...

Covey would finish off by saying, 'So what does that tell you about time?' to which they'd answer something such as, 'Regardless of how much you do, in your day-to-day life, there's always more you can squeeze in.' At which point he'd say, 'No! That's exactly what it isn't about. Unless you fit the *big rocks* in first, how on earth can you fit them in later?'

And that's the essence of his *compass* message (and something **Business Geniuses** do well). Work out your true North and prioritise that above all else, rather than getting caught up in the day-to-day 'tyranny of the urgent'.

STEPHEN COVEY
(1932 - 2012)

USEFUL TIPS AND ESCAPE STRATEGIES

So if you want to **UP!** your time management, here are three practical tips and techniques that can help:

1 STOP DOING THINGS

It's simply amazing how many **Business Geniuses** manage to achieve so much in such a limited period of time.

Look at Timothy Ferriss, for example (the author of *The 4-Hour Work Week: Escape the 9–5, live anywhere and join the new rich*). He worked out an ingenious way of delegating virtually everything he does, so he now makes far more money than he used to, doing far less work.

Or, how about the famous children's author Enid Blyton? In her lifetime she evidently wrote 186 novels, 223 character books, 267 education books, 179 reaction books, 153 continuation books and 884 short story series.

Now – leaving a discussion about the quality of those books firmly to one side – the point is there's no way she'd have been able to write them all if she hadn't *stopped* doing others things!

So if it's effective time management you're after, keep on asking yourself what *you* could potentially *stop doing* because, as time management expert Jan Jasper makes clear: 'Saying *no* to some activities is the only way you can say *yes* to what you really value.'

With this in mind, let's just forget tips 2 and 3 …

BUSINESS GENIUS IN ACTION: NEXT STEPS …

In summary, if you want to **UP!** your time management skills, here's how:

❶ **P**inpoint what is realistic and unrealistic time management (because you can't do everything, and not everything's worth doing).

❷ **I**nvestigate how time management is really all about psychology (otherwise it's easy to assume that time management issues can automatically be fixed with a snazzy new time-planner, yet 'Script Theory' suggests it often runs deeper than that).

❸ **L**everage the effectiveness of the 4 Es: *emergency* time, *enrichment* time, *entrapment* time and *empty* time (because – as Covey suggested – all actitivies can basically be divided up into four main categories, depending upon their varying levels of importance and urgency, and Enrichment time is the one that's most likely to take us to new heights … for these are *the big rocks*!).

4 Orchestrate a plan for becoming the PILOT of your own time (for, unless you take control of the 86,400 seconds in your day, almost by default, there's every chance those 86,400 seconds will start to take control of you).

5 Target what you're going to stop doing (by remembering Jan Jasper's pearl of business wisdom: 'Saying *no* to some activities is the only way you can say *yes* to what you really value').

UP!SPIRATION
'Time stays long enough for those who use it.'
Leonardo Da Vinci

PART 2
GET ON WITH OTHERS

'Business is about people.'
Tom Peters

UP! YOUR
INFLUENCE

The sixth **B**lock and **L**imitation to **Business Genius** is **insufficient influence**. This doesn't mean we have to have the charisma of JFK, or the hypnotic powers of Rasputin, to excel at work. It simply means our ability to influence others is a supremely useful skill and, without it, we're unlikely to soar too high in the world of business.

So what's the secret?

Well, weirdly enough, it's reminding ourselves that **effective influence** is *not* just about getting others to do what *we* want them to do.

On the contrary.

As Dale Carnegie – who wrote the 1937 classic *How to Win Friends and Influence People* – smartly observed: 'There is only one way to get anybody to do anything, yes, just one way, and that is making the other person *want* to do it.'

If we want to become **Genius** influencers, the trick is to view a situation from the other people's perspective *before* we expect them to see it from ours. In other words, instead of being rigidly self-centred, we need to be more *flexible* (in our thinking and behaviours) so we can *flow* …

In fact, that's precisely where the words *influence* and affluence come from.

Back in Roman times *influere* meant 'to flow into' so, when we influence other people, our thoughts, ideas and opinions literally flow into them and, when we're influenced *by* other people, their thoughts, ideas and opinions literally flow into us.

Insufficient influencers, however, frequently overlook the value of *flow*!

As a result – according to brainwashing and mind technician expert Kathleen Taylor – they accidentally trigger a part of the human brain called the prefrontal cortex (the PFC), which enables us to stop and think when we feel we're being tricked, taken advantage of and dragged in a direction we're reluctant to go in.

Forgive me if this sounds like psychological gobbledegook, but it's important: if you've ever come across someone in the workplace who's refusing to budge an inch, and is as stubborn as a mule, this is why!

So, if you want to become a highly skilled influencer you'll need to *flow* around other people's PFCs (rather than bang into them).

So here are two top tips to help you achieve this:

❶ **Build rapport.** Invest time in building *rapport* (i.e. harmonious social interaction) with the person you want to influence. In other words, *actively listen* to them, take a genuine interest in what they're saying, and do your best to mirror and match their words and body language as much as possible (without sounding like a parrot, or prancing around like Marcel Marceau, the **Genius** mime artist). Besides, who would you rather do business with? Someone you like and trust – because they speak your language – or someone you don't? By the way, if you really want to master the subtle nuances of rapport-building, I suggest you read plenty of neuro-linguistic programming (NLP) books because they often excel in this area. If you're simply looking for a quick shortcut, however, just imagine that the person you aim to influence has an invisible sign over their head that reads: 'Help me feel important!' Help them do this – honestly and authentically – and you can bet your bottom dollar the rest will *flow* from there …

❷ **Project passion.** It could be argued that teaching is one of the most uber-influential professions on the planet. What separates *great teaching* from *average teaching*, however? Well, evidently, it's not just subject knowledge or decades of experience … it's *passion*! So please bear this in mind if you want to **UP!** your influence at work. Get *passionate* about whatever it is you're selling, making or doing (and influencing others will start to become a whole lot easier). After all, would the Rolling Stones have been so influential if they hadn't been so *passionate* about rock 'n' roll? Would Steven Spielberg have been so influential if he hadn't been so *passionate* about the world of film-making? And would Enzo Ferrari (1898–1988) have been so influential if he hadn't been so *passionate* about auto design and racing cars?

UP! YOUR INFLUENCE NUGGET

Many **Business Geniuses** have been hugely influential over the years.

Think of J. P. Morgan, for example, and his influence on investment banking; or William Shakespeare and his influence on theatre and literature; or Igor Sikorsky and his influence on helicopter travel. Likewise, if we glance around the globe – from India to China to Spain – it's easy to see Lakshmi Mittal's influence on the steel industry, or Wang Jianlin's influence on real estate, or the founders of Zara, Rosalia Mera and Amancio Ortega's influence on high-street fashion ...

Few **Business Geniuses**, however, even come close to the far-reaching influence of Walt Disney!

From his many magical movies (for which he received 22 Oscars) to his innovative theme parks, and from his influence on everything from animated computer games to popular culture, no wonder Disney's biographer Neal Gabler once wrote: 'He changed the world.'

Walt Disney's **Genius**, however, might never have seen the light of day if he'd listened to his critics and allowed them to tread on his dreams. Back in the 1930s, for example, dissenters of his *Snow White* project referred to it as 'Disney's Folly', because they considered the idea of a full-length animated feature film (which had never been attempted before) to be utterly absurd! They naturally assumed the bright colours would be too distracting, and that children wouldn't be able to concentrate for such a long period of time. Disney, however, refused to be influenced by this way of thinking, and went on to create his multi-billion dollar entertainment empire. No wonder Disney once said: 'I only hope that we don't lose sight of one thing – that it was all started by a mouse.' Yup. If Mickey Mouse could be this influential, who knows what you could do?

USEFUL TIPS AND ESCAPE STRATEGIES

Against this backdrop, here are three useful tips and escape strategies you may want to explore to help you **UP!** your influence:

1 ALWAYS SAY 'BECAUSE'

Back in the 1970s a Harvard psychologist called Professor Ellen Langer conducted an experiment with people in an office who were queuing up to use a photocopying machine (as they did in those days!).

An actor would run up to the front and queue barge, but use different excuses. When he ran up and said, 'Excuse me, I have five pages. May I use the photocopier?' he was 60 per cent successful. By contrast, when he ran up and said the same thing, but added, 'because I'm in a rush', he was 94 per cent successful.

Langer's key finding, however, emerged after the line, 'Excuse me, I have five pages. May I use the photocopier because I have to make some copies' was used.

Amazingly, this turned out to be 93 per cent successful, even though it was blatantly obvious that they'd need to 'make some copies' if they were going to use the photocopier. This led Langer to conclude that it was the word *because* that made the crucial difference, *not* what came after it.

So bear this in mind next time you want to influence someone.

Give people a *because* before they ask for one. So, instead of saying, 'Please can I have three minutes of your time' say,

'Please can I have three minutes of your time because ...' It won't always work, but it'll definitely help *because* we usually like to know why we're being asked to do something before we end up saying 'yes' to it!

2 GIVE TO GAIN

Influence guru Robert Cialdini highlights how there are six *'weapons of influence'* to sway people's thinking.

For example, sales people often use the weapon of *scarcity*, e.g. they let a customer know it's the last one left in the shop to prompt them to snap it up quickly, before someone else does.

Sports marketing professionals, meanwhile, often rely on the weapon of *liking*, e.g. they leverage the popularity and *likeability* of sporting heroes to champion certain brands, to tempt their fans to wear the same sunglasses or football boots, too.

One of the most widely used weapons of them all, however, is *reciprocity*, i.e. the principle of 'we get what we give'.

Ever noticed, for example, how, if you buy someone a drink in a bar, they're more likely to buy you one? Or, if you help a colleague at work, they're more likely to help you in return? Of course it doesn't always work – because some people are pathologically selfish – however, keep giving this a go and see where it takes you.

Besides, *reciprocal* arrangements have been going on in business since time immemorial. Take the Royal Navy, for example, where back in the 1800s sailors used to say, 'You scratch my back, and I'll scratch yours.'

The reason they said this was because naval discipline was brutal back then, and sailors could easily get whipped for doing the slightest thing wrong. On a long sea journey, however, if you were given orders to whip someone else's back (with a whip called a cat-o'-nine-tails, which used to leave nasty 'scratch' marks), sooner or later you'd probably be the one to make a mistake, and they'd end up 'scratching' you. So, in terms of influence, sailors soon realised it was smarter to come to a *reciprocal* arrangement: go easy with me, and I'll go easy with you …

3 SWAP THE BAIT

Finally, we need to remember that *influence* and *motivation* are closely connected. Or, to put it another way, if someone's demotivated (i.e. they lack hope and desire) influencing them is going to be hard work!

So, why not give yourself a break, and find out what really motivates the other person *before* you attempt to influence them. If they're motivated by *money*, for example, make sure the bait on your hook is money; if they're motivated by *recognition*, make sure the bait on your hook is recognition; if they're motivated by spending more time on activities of their choice, make sure the bait on your hook is an opportunity for them to spend more time on activities of their choice. Yes, it might sound manipulative. However, it's really more about *connecting* (or what persuasion expert James Borg calls 'listening with your heart') than manipulating. Or, to put it another way, it's doing what message strategist Chris St Hilaire refers to as 'recognising their reality'.

For, as David Lloyd George – the former British Prime Minister (1916–1922) – used to say: 'Bait the hook to suit the fish!'

BUSINESS GENIUS IN ACTION: NEXT STEPS ...

In summary, if you want to **UP!** your influence, here's how:

❶ **P**inpoint the difference rapport can make (for people in business usually don't need a good talking to, they need a good listening to, so focus on entering into *their* world first, before you expect them to enter into yours).

❷ **I**nvestigate smarter ways of giving (and, no, this doesn't mean giving dodgy back-handers! It simply means reciprocation can often be a highly powerful weapon of influence because, if your colleagues know you are there for them – as Brent and Dent make clear in their book *The Leader's Guide to Influence* – they'll be more likely to be there for you).

❸ **L**everage the power of passion (because – as we saw with Ferrari – passion is often contagious when it comes to selling business products, services and ideas. Besides, if you can't influence yourself, how on earth can you be expected to influence others?).

❹ **O**rchestrate a plan to 'Bait the hook to suit the fish' (for when it comes to effective influence there is no magic wand or one-size-fits-all solution that will work for everyone. The secret is to keep *flexing* your approach, and concentrate on what *others* most want).

❺ **T**arget the word 'because' (*because* it will help you to fly around people's PFCs! So, instead of saying, 'Please can you finish this report by the end of Thursday', say 'Please can you finish this report by the end of Thursday because I promised the senior management team I'd let them see it first thing Friday morning.' It'll be far more convincing!).

UP!SPIRATION

'The key to successful leadership today is influence, not authority.'

Ken Blanchard (American author and management expert)

UP! YOUR
IMPACT

The seventh **B**lock and **L**imitation to **Business Genius** is **negative impact**.

And negative impact usually happens for two reasons:

❶ There's not enough wham! (In other words, we make such a *soft* impression on others, we *barely* get noticed or remembered.)

❷ There's too much wham! (In other words, we make such a *hard* impression on others, we *do* get noticed, and we *do* get remembered, but for all the *wrong* reasons.)

Positive impact is all about striking a healthy balance, so we strike into others in a strong, yet not over-strong, way.

Unfortunately, however, this can be tricky, because it's not always easy to *know* how we do come across to other people.

In a business meeting, for example, *we* might think we're being precise, but *others* might think we're being picky; *we* might think we're being silently attentive, but *others* might think we're being aloof; or *we* might think we've got an amazing winning smile, but *others* might be grossed out by the spinach in our teeth.

Similarly, we don't always *know* how impactful things can be.

Take the airline industry, for example. Recent research has shown that the number one threat to airline security is not terrorism, or mechanical error, but pilot tiredness. Evidently, the impact of a poor night's sleep on a pilot's concentration and decision making can be hugely significant.

Or consider the impact of the chocolate wafer bar KitKat in Japan. Purely by chance the name KitKat (which was an abbreviation of **Ch**ris**t**opher **Cat**ling – the owner of a pie shop in eighteenth-century England where the Kit-Kat Club used to meet) sparked massive commercial success in Japan because it sounds remarkably similar to *kitto katsu*, the Japanese phrase for 'you will definitely succeed'.

Consequently, millions of Japanese not only buy KitKat chocolate bars as snacks, but also as gifts, too!

So if you aspire to **UP!** your impact, please be mindful of 'how little things can make a big difference' (as the impactful author Malcolm Gladwell surmises in his millennium bestseller, *The Tipping Point: How little things can make a big difference*).

One of the 'little things' Gladwell pointed out was how a 'single, breakthrough insight' – by the **Business Genius** Joan Ganz Cooney back in the 1960s – ended up having a massive impact on literacy levels around the world.

TV producer Cooney believed, 'If you can hold the attention of children, you can educate them,' and her **Genius** TV show *Sesame Street* went on to be living proof of that!

In the work *you* do, keep remembering that positive impact is as much about the *micro* as the *macro*, from the way you shake someone's hand for the first time, to the way you look someone in the eye.

I was once told, for example, how a young recruit at a large bank lost their job because they wrote, '31 June' on an important document. Why? Because there are clearly only 30 days in June, and this tiny error seriously undermined that bank's credibility with one of their major clients.

On a more positive note, however, you may want to consider this.

One of the most impactful things you can ever do in business is say thank you (a *genuine* thank you) for a job well done. Research has shown, for example, that organisations with a ratio of positive feedback to negative feedback of 3:1 significantly outperform those where managerial praise and recognition is hard to come by, and where managerial criticism and fault-finding are day-to-day routine.

So, please bear in mind that – when it comes to impact – the world of work doesn't have to be the immovable, implacable place we often assume it to be. As Gladwell writes: 'With the slightest push – in just the right place – it can be tipped'...

MALCOLM GLADWELL

UP! YOUR IMPACT
NUGGET

Most people have never heard of Edwin Drake.

Likewise, they've no idea why Sunday 28 August 1859 turned out to be one of the most impactful days in history!

The chain of events Drake set in motion that day, however, is simply mind-blowing. What did he do? Well, he used a little **Genius** thinking to come up with a *new way* of finding *oil*.

Evidently – according to author Stephen Howarth in his book *A Century in Oil: The 'Shell' Transport and Trading Company 1897–1997* – before Drake it was *assumed* that the best way to extract oil involved digging pits or 'skimming natural seepings from the surfaces of streams'.

In other words, it was *assumed* that oil couldn't be obtained quickly, easily, or in 'commercially viable quantities'; by contrast, it could be obtained only in small amounts, and very slowly, like patiently waiting for the sap to ooze out of trees.

Drake, however, who had originally worked on the railways, wondered what might happen if he drilled for oil. So, on that specific day in 1859, he used a rickety derrick in Pennsylvania to drill 69 feet down and ... whoosh! He not only struck oil, but he kick-started the entire oil industry, which currently employs more people than any other industry on the planet!

Not only that. If we think of oil as 'the great enabler' – as Howarth describes it – it's hard to think of a business that hasn't been impacted upon by Drake's breakthrough moment in some way. From planes, trains and automobiles to computers, dresses, skis, glasses, guitar strings, golf balls, crayons, ballpoint pens, deodorant, footballs, cameras, paint and even aspirin, oil is now used in over 6,000 different items!

USEFUL TIPS AND ESCAPE STRATEGIES

If you're eager to **UP!** your impact, here are three practical tips and strategies that can help:

1 ALWAYS START WELL

One of the biggest clichés of impact training courses is that, 'You never get a second chance to make a first impression.' Unfortunately, this strategic insight (which psychologists label 'the primacy effect') is all too true!

So, whether you're an entrepreneur who's about to make an 'elevator pitch' to potential investors, a new manager who's about to say 'hello' to their new team, or a leader who's about to deliver that uplifting keynote speech at the annual conference, make sure you get off to a **great start**.

This is because first impressions often have what Massachusetts Institute of Technology's Edward Lorenz called 'the butterfly effect' (i.e. a ripple effect that starts as something minor – like the flapping of a butterfly's wings – and ends up as something major, like a tidal wave on the far end of the world).

That's not to say you automatically have to leap to the other extreme and make a grand entrance like Cleopatra (who famously emerged out of an unfurled carpet at the feet of Mark Antony when they met for the first time!); it simply means that, if you want to 'impress your way to success' (as Vickers, Banister and Smith would say), keep reminding yourself that Shakespeare was only half right when he wrote the immortal words 'All's well that ends well' …

2 USE 'LISTENING EYES'

One of the most effective ways of gauging the impact you have on others is simply to **listen with your eyes**. Or, to put it another way, don't just listen to what people say, watch what they do, too.

If you're giving a business presentation, for example, be alert to your audience's non-verbal clues. If one person happens to yawn, for example, it could be they're just tired after an exhausting inter-continental flight. If everyone's yawning, though, there's a good chance you'll need to change gear, instantly!

Presentation skills experts call this 'Hooking The Curtain Up', and it's vital if you want to deliver more impactful presentations.

All you have to do is something – anything – to help break the pattern! Gently clap your hands together to emphasise your point (which will wake them up a bit) or throw a prop in the air (without hurting anyone) or give your delegates a question to discuss with the person sitting next to them. Put simply, make a switch. Even walking to a different part of the stage can help, too.

By the way, remember to listen with your eyes at the end of a work engagement, too, because – when it comes to impact – it's *not* so much what you take away with you that counts ... it's what you leave behind!

3 SHARPEN YOUR 'BRAND'

Like it or not, every single one of us is a 'brand'.

That's to say, from the clothes we wear to the words we speak, we're the human equivalent of a packet of Oreo cookies, Nike trainers, or perhaps even a red Ducati motorbike.

Winston Churchill's bowler hat, for example, was an indispensable part of his image (as was his bow tie and cigar). Likewise, Psy – the South Korean pop star – used a highly original and impactful dance routine in his *Gangnam Style* video to help turn his song into the biggest YouTube hit ever (watched by over 2 billion viewers as of May 2014!). And, if you think about it, even knights in shining armour used to wear coats of arms because, with their helmets on, it was the only way soldiers on the battle field could tell them apart.

In this respect, keep asking yourself if your personal brand is as impactful as you need it to be (or, if not, what you could potentially do to sharpen your offering).

After all, as Jim Rohn – the **Genius** personal development guru – once said, if you want to make real progress in business, you've got to 'work harder on yourself than you do at your job'. Likewise, it's also why Tom Peters – the infamous co-author of *In Search of Excellence* – argues: 'The only job security [in the modern world] is to make sure that you're more valuable tomorrow, than you are today!' So keep building your own brand, or rebrand yourself if necessary, so you **stand out** as a core competent.

Whilst we're on the subject of personal branding, however, please bear in mind that successful brands are built upon trust. Or, as Ian Robertson – the head of sales and marketing at BMW – said in a recent TV interview: 'What is a brand? A brand is essentially a promise. A promise of innovation, a promise of outstanding design, a promise of safety ...' So, whatever you do in business, be as authentic as you can be, because it's often nigh on impossible to rescue a brand that's gone toxic, because people won't trust it any more.

Finally, here's a fourth top tip (a bonus tip) to help you **UP!** your impact.

4 DECLUTTER YOUR MIND

It's often said – by management consultancies such as Kepner-Tregoe – that 'effective action follows clear thinking.'

So if it's **Business Genius** impact you're after, it's important to remember that high impact in business is virtually impossible if our thinking is all over the place. Or, as Chris Brogan and Julien Smith – the authors of *The Impact Equation* – put it: 'Are you making things happen, or just making a noise?'

Also, here's a bit of golden advice that productivity expert David Allen suggests in his book *Getting Things Done*: 'Use your mind to think about things, rather than of them.'

In other words, create a trusted system (of folders and lists) to help you get what's on your mind, off your mind, in a systematic and organised way. That way you can create some sharper boundaries between your thoughts, much like the barbed wire that **Business Genius** and Illinois farmer Joseph Glidden invented in 1874.

Once again, it might sound blindingly obvious but the ability to **clear your head** is vital if you want to sharpen your business impact! After all, sharper thinking didn't do Glidden much harm. He became one of the richest men in America on the back of it!

BUSINESS GENIUS IN ACTION: NEXT STEPS ...

In summary, if you want to **UP!** your impact, here's how:

❶ Pinpoint where too much wham! stops, and not enough wham! begins (to help you 'strike into' others in a strong, yet not over-strong, way).

❷ Investigate how little things can often have a big impact (as we illustrated with KitKat in Japan, Cooney with *Sesame Street* and Edwin Drake with his ingenious idea of drilling for oil).

❸ Leverage the power of starting well (because, as we all know, we'll never get a second chance to make a first impression).

❹ Orchestrate a plan for sharpening your personal brand (to ensure you get noticed, and remembered, for all the best reasons).

⑤ **T**arget clear thinking (so you can use your mind to think about things rather than of them, otherwise your thinking will end up cluttered, and you'll simply make a noise rather than make things happen).

UP!SPIRATION
'The only limit to your impact is your imagination and commitment.'
Tony Robbins (American life coach, self-help author and motivational speaker)

UP! YOUR
ASSERTIVENESS

The eighth **B**lock and **L**imitation to **Business Genius** is **awkward assertiveness**.

This awkwardness, however, is perhaps to be expected, because no one is born assertive.

On the contrary.

If you were to snatch a toy away from a young child who was enjoying playing with it, for example, what do you think would happen?

Well, the chances are they'd:

→ cry (i.e. go **passive**);

→ have a temper tantrum (i.e. go **aggressive**);

→ peer up at you with those pleading eyes (i.e. go **manipulative**); or

→ say nothing to your face, but then sneakily snatch it back again when you're looking the other way (i.e. go **passive aggressive**).

Anyway, the point is, what they're highly unlikely to say is:

'Excuse me, when you took my toy away from me like that, I felt sad and angry because I was enjoying playing with it. With this in mind, I'd appreciate it if you could return it instantly. In future, if you would like to borrow my toy, I suggest we discuss this rationally, calmly and in advance next time, so we can move towards a mutually beneficial outcome. In what ways could we potentially work together to help this happen?'

Why?

Because assertiveness is a social skill, and this means it's a skill we need to learn.

And here lies the problem. Who on earth are we supposed to learn it from? Our parents? Our teachers? Our friends? (Mmm ... no wonder so many businesses are fraught with people problems!)

Anyway, leaving that Pandora's Box firmly closed for now, let's take a look at three key learning points that can help you to **UP!** your assertiveness.

POINT 1 **WHAT?**

What does assertiveness mean? Well, according to Sue Bishop in her book *Develop Your Assertiveness*, it basically means **rights**. That's to say, it means 'standing up for your own rights without violating the rights of other people.'

Passive people, for example (like Stan Laurel of *Laurel and Hardy* fame) frequently ignore their own rights; aggressive people (like Sonny Corleone in Martin Scorsese's *The Godfather*) frequently ignore others' rights; assertive people, however, (like the BBC's David Dimbleby, who's been diplomatically chairing the political debate programme *Question Time* for many years) frequently respect both.

POINT 2 **WHEN?**

When is it appropriate to be assertive in business? The simple answer is **often, but *not* always**! Sometimes, you might need to be a little more aggressive (especially if you want to achieve aggressive sales results or 'Swim with the sharks (without being eaten alive)', as business author Harvey Mackay would say). Alternatively, at other times, you might need to be a little more passive (especially if you work in a 'Yes, Chef!' culture, where assertiveness is viewed as mutiny, and potentially career-limiting). Please be aware that 'assertiveness', as Sue Bishop also states, 'is always a *choice* of behaviour.' And this means, one of your rights includes your right not to be assertive! After all, Tom Cruise was amazingly forthright in the movie *Jerry Maguire*, but not everyone welcomed his refreshing honesty!

POINT 3 **HOW?**

How can assertiveness best be achieved? Well, we'll explore this in more detail in a minute. Ultimately, however, the trick is to **talk in paragraphs** (as hinted at earlier). Yup. If you want to be assertive, bear in mind that it's virtually always the *longest* option. If you want to be aggressive, for example, you can probably say what you want to say in two or three words like 'Get stuffed!' or 'Go to hell!' By contrast, if you want to go passive, you could probably get away without saying anything (and silently nod in agreement). Assertiveness, however, tends to take the most time …

PASSIVE   AGGRESSIVE   ASSERTIVE!

UP! YOUR ASSERTIVENESS NUGGET

In 1976 a housewife called Anita Roddick – from a little town called Littlehampton in the South of England – was left to bring up her two children alone while her husband Gordon trekked across the Americas.

Let's face it, Roddick could easily have turned passive and wallowed in self-pity, but she didn't. Likewise, she could easily have turned manipulative, and put emotional pressure on her husband to curtail his trip immediately, but Roddick had brighter ideas.

She decided to set up a brand new business called The Body Shop (to help her pay the bills) instead, and her innovative cosmetics concept went on to become a resounding success with its '2,045 stores serving more than 77 million customers in 51 different markets in 25 different languages and across 12 time zones.'

In this light, it's fair to say that Anita Roddick – the 'capitalist with a conscience' (to quote journalist James Macintyre of *The Independent*) – was a prime example of 'assertiveness in action' for three main reasons:

→ Firstly, she wasn't afraid to stand up for the rights of *working mothers*, demonstrating how it was perfectly possible for a mother to pay her way in the world by tapping into the power of her ingenuity.

→ Secondly, she wasn't afraid to stand up for the rights of *animals*, too, choosing only to sell products that hadn't been tested on them.

→ Finally – as we discover in her 1991 autobiography *Body and Soul* – she wasn't afraid to stand up for the rights of all *ethical entrepreneurs*, by championing the idea of 'profits from principles', assertively stating: 'We are proving that you can be successful and still keep your sense of soul, you can make a profit and still be a force for social change …'

USEFUL TIPS AND ESCAPE STRATEGIES

If you genuinely want to **UP!** the quality of your assertiveness, here are three practical tips and strategies that can help:

1 ALWAYS USE 'ISA'

ISA is a simple three-step process – recommended by Cathy Birch in her book *Asserting Your Self: How to feel confident about getting more from life* – that stands for **I**dentify, **S**tate, **A**sk, and here's how it works:

→ Firstly, you **identify** the specific behaviour you're not too happy about (because this will help you to keep personal remarks out of it).

→ Secondly, you **state** the effect it's had – or is having – on you (because this will enable you to steer clear of arguments about the truth, for you'll be describing the situation only as *you* see it, from *your* perspective).

→ Thirdly, you **ask** for the change you'd most like to happen (because clear signposting will make it infinitely easier for the other person to see what it is you want them to do differently).

And that's basically it, rather like this:

→ **I**dentify: 'When you were late for our meeting last Thursday, which started at 2.30 pm …'

→ **S**tate: ' I felt let down because I was relying on you being there to introduce the new project to the rest of the team …'

→ **A**sk: 'In future, please can you let me know if you are going to be running late, so I can plan around it …'

By the way, ISA can also be very useful if you're a manager who's just about to give an appraisal or performance review to someone who's not great at taking feedback, because it can help you to structure your conversation in a systematic and non-confrontational way.

2 TARGET THE MIDDLE

In Sweden, there's a wonderful word – *lagom* – which basically means 'not too much' and 'not too little'. And in many ways this sums up assertiveness.

Assertiveness is all about keeping everything you say, and everything you do, bang in the middle. And this is because assertiveness is all about the middle ego state (i.e. the adult ego state), which is all about being rational, objective, neutral and keeping emotions well and truly out of it!

Like *lagom*, therefore, it means not being too loud, and not being too quiet.

It means 'keeping your head on straight' (as they say in psychology) because aggressive people tend to jut their heads forward, whereas manipulative people tend to tilt their heads to one side.

And here's a weird one. I've come across assertiveness experts who suggest we 'keep our eyebrows straight!' Yup, if you think about it, when we get angry our eyebrows tend to end up looking like the letter V, yet if we go passive they tend to look more like an arch or a rainbow ...

3 FORGET POWER GAMES

There are times when it's relatively *easy* to be assertive. For example, if you know your subject, you're working with amazingly approachable people, or if there are no grey areas, such as when you have the law behind you, like an environmental health officer (who has the authority to close down a restaurant instantly if the owner fails to comply with specific standards).

Other times, however, it can be *hard*. For example, if you're dealing with someone who's intimidating, or unpredictable, if you feel like a fish out of water, if you need to give bad news, or perhaps if you're so nice you don't like to say no.

Whatever the context, if you're keen to gain 'mastery in the emotional domain' (as Daniel Goleman writes about in his 1995 classic *Emotional Intelligence*) it's a good idea to have your own strategy for staying centred in highly challenging circumstances.

So here's one that might intrigue you: **always think Gurkha!**

Yes, I know it sounds a bit crazy, but mental visualisation (or what psychologists call visual motor behaviour rehearsal) can often help if you want to come across as appropriately powerful in a tense situation.

After all, why is it that ex-Gurkha soldiers are increasingly being recruited as security guards by top business people in the UK and elsewhere? Well, largely because these brave kukri-wielding fighters from the steep hills of Nepal appear to excel at handling conflict situations asssertively (rather than aggressively like a nightclub bouncer, passively, or manipulatively).

In other words, they're able to stay strong and stand up for their rights under extreme pressure, yet also to remain restrained, too. For as Dilli Gurung – an ex-Gurkha and experienced security guard I know – recently told me, much of this assertiveness comes from a blend of honesty, discipline and pride: 'We Gurkhas proudly remember and respect our prestige, and this prestige gives us a big moral to work strongly and effectively.'

So, please bear this in mind, within the context of the work you do: If you want to **UP!** your assertiveness, value who you are and value what you do.

Or, as Cathy Birch makes clear: 'Assertiveness begins with a sense of self-worth. When we value ourselves we have no need for power games.'

To round up, however, here are few extra insights, which may also be of interest:

→ Please don't *assume* that passives are so meek and gentle that they are never angry. (Passives can often be very angry – inside – but simply do not show it.)

→ Please don't *assume* that aggressives are only ever loud, red in the face and point a lot, like the monster boss in *The Devil Wears Prada*. (Aggression can take many shapes and forms. Some people, for example, can be aggressive with silence, or with an icy cold stare. In fact – according to Roberta Cava in her book *Dealing with Difficult People* – everything from 'gossip' to 'sarcasm', and even eye-ball rolling, can be indirect forms of 'aggression' in the workplace!)

BUSINESS GENIUS IN ACTION: NEXT STEPS ...

In summary, if you want to **UP!** your assertiveness, here's how:

❶ **P**inpoint what rights you, and others, have at work (to help you appreciate what's acceptable behaviour, and what isn't).

❷ **I**nvestigate what assertiveness is *not* (for the sharper your understanding of what makes passivity, aggression and manipulation so different, the better placed you'll be to act on it).

❸ **L**everage the power of ISA (by *identifying* the problem behaviour you're not happy with, *stating* the effect it's having on you and your team, and then *asking* for the change you'd most like to see in future. Yes, it'll definitely seem robotic, and you'll end up having to talk in paragraphs but, if done well, it can help).

❹ **O**rchestrate a plan to 'think Gurkha!' (so you can avoid petty power games and develop your sense of self).

❺ **T**arget the middle (by keeping everything you do and say in the middle, including your eyebrows!).

And, once again, remember that too much assertiveness can be career-limiting, so please choose your moment.

UP!SPIRATION
'Courage is found in unlikely places.'
J. R. R. Tolkien (English writer, poet, philologist and university professor)

UP! YOUR COMMUNICATION SKILLS

The ninth **B**lock and **L**imitation to **Business Genius** are **clumsy communication skills**. And they're often clumsy because people make the mistake of thinking: effective communication = 'the transfer of information from sender to receiver.'

It doesn't.

Effective communication (as Dr Sandi Mann highlights in her book *Psychology Goes to Work*) = 'when the sender creates a message that is *understood* by the receiver.'

Admittedly, they sound strikingly similar, but here's why they're different:

Non-Genius communicators *boldly broadcast* what they want to say (irrespective of the type of person they're communicating with). That's why, in a business context, you'll often hear them mutter, 'How many more times do I need to tell them?' or 'They just don't get it!!!'

Genius communicators, however, consciously *tailor* their message so it resonates as much as possible with their target audience. Look at BankAmericard, for example.

Back in the 1960s, and early 1970s, this US credit card company found its name worked perfectly well in the USA. But, around the world, it was a different story.

This is why, in 1977, its founder – Dee Hock – came up with an ingenious new name for it: Visa.

And why did he choose this name?

Well, firstly because Visa is a word that's understood in multiple languages and countries across the globe; secondly, Visa is a word that stands for universal acceptance.

Likewise, here's a stroke of **Business Genius** the London and North Eastern Railway (LNER) came up with in 1923.

The company was in its infancy and keen to find a cunningly clever way to promote itself with the public, and also to put one of its key competitors – Great Western – in the shade.

So, what did it do?

Well, according to the author Andrew Roden, LNER decided to relabel one of its trains – train No.1472 (which, basically, was just a 'column in the timetable') – and in the process it ended up creating a legend: The Flying Scotsman!

Suddenly, by using the **Genius** of communication and an 'evocative, resounding [new] name', which suggested both speed and freedom, it was able to transform the regular 10 am train (from King's Cross to Edinburgh) into living metal.

So, whether you're communicating face-to-face, via email, or speaking at a conference, please remember this: *what* you say no doubt matters, but *how* you say it often matters more.

And, if you're after some living proof of this, the world of business books is a pretty good place to start.

Back in 2005, Dubner and Levitt could easily have written one of those stodgy textbooks on economics, but it wouldn't exactly have flown off the shelves. So, instead, they repackaged profound economic insights in an accessible way to help fascinate and interest a mainstream audience. The result? The global bestseller *Freakonomics*.

Likewise, in 2012, was the reading public beating down the door for yet another book on body language? No, not really. But then along came a supersmart body language book with the catchy title – *Spy The Lie* (written by four former CIA agents) – and suddenly readers lapped it up.

And so the list of highly resonant titles goes on, from Steven Silbiger's *The 10-Day MBA* to Jim Collins's *Good to Great*.

Next time you want your communication to connect, bear in mind: 'It's not what you're selling, it's what they're buying' that ultimately counts …

UP! YOUR COMMUNICATION SKILLS NUGGET

It could be argued that David Ogilvy – the co-founder of the advertising agency Ogilvy & Mather – was one of the top **Business Genius** communicators of the twentieth century.

After all, back in the 1960s, his drive and talent helped attract 19 clients (ranging from Schweppes to Shell) whose revenues actually *exceeded* the revenue of the UK Government!

Ultimately, however, central to Ogilvy's success was the view that 'you cannot bore people into buying' something.

On the contrary.

As he spelled out – in his autobiography *Confessions of an Advertising Man* – 'Advertising is a business of words', and those words need to help a client's offering to be 'heard above the crowd'.

Some of his most famous ads – such as the eye-patched 'Man in the Hathaway Shirt' probably mean zilch to the modern generation. However, if you're interested, take a good look at his 'Guinness Guide to Oysters', for example, to appreciate how deceptively powerful his factual advertising ('the more you tell, the more you sell') could be.

Likewise, consider the **Genius** advertising copy he once provided for Rolls-Royce as a mini-masterclass in the power of persuasive communication: 'At 60 miles an hour the loudest noise in this new Rolls-Royce comes from the electric clock ...'

DAVID OGILVY (1911-1999)

If you want to **UP!** your communication skills, here are three useful tips and strategies that can help:

1 KNOW YOUR AUDIENCE

Psychometric research indicates that different people prefer to communicate in different ways.

With this in mind, here's something I created called **READ** (which is basically a distillation, and amalgamation, of several psychometrics ranging from MBTI to HBDI, and SDI to psychologists Merrill and Reid's Social Styles Model) which can help you to *connect* more effectively with whoever you want to *connect* with.

Here's how it works.

Although human beings are far too complex to squeeze into psychological boxes, if there were four boxes we could squeeze more or less everyone into (to make it easier for us to READ them like a book) these would be those four:

R: Results-orientated people, as the name suggests, are primarily interested in results. They're not interested in fluff or waffle. They're super-driven, often impatient, and want you to get straight to the point (rather like Sir Alex Ferguson, Gordon Ramsay and Lord Alan Sugar, whose autobiography *What You See is What You Get!*, says it all really).

To communicate with an R, don't bore them with the details. Use bullet points and snappy one-page summaries. Best of all, talk results!

E: Emotions-orientated people are primarily interested in emotions. They're the caring ones (who Merrill and Reid referred to as 'amiables') who are genuinely interested in how you are, and what you've been up to. Think Joanna Lumley (the former *Avenger*), for example, David Schwimmer (of *Friends*), or maybe even a variety of social entrepreneurs who are guided as much by ethics as by profit.

To communicate with an E, simply show a genuine interest in how they're feeling and, if they're going through painful change at work, let them know you're there to provide help and support.

A: Abracadabra-orientated people are primarily interested in the magic and zing of business (and often tend to be very good at standing up and giving entertaining presentations and coming up with ideas during brainstorms). Think Jonathan Ross, Eddie Murphy, Tony Blair, Ruby Wax, etc. etc.

To communicate with an A, keep it interesting and sparky, and value their input.

D: Data-orientated people are primarily interested in data. Or, more to the point, they get their comfort from data (and therefore dislike things being too vague or imprecise). So think Sherlock Holmes, Spock from *Star Trek*, or countless scientists, academics, accountants and IT experts, who love the details.

To communicate with a D, simply make sure you're thorough, and that your research, facts and figures are perfectly precise and exact.

Admittedly, this probably sounds simplistic (especially as most of us are a blend of all four). However, there's definitely something in it, as they say.

When my first book *Gen!us* came out, for example, I got a real sense of READ in action. An E, for example, would say something like, 'Well done. That's a great achievement. Your dad would've been very proud!'; an A would say, 'Wow! Fab bright yellow cover!'; a D would say, 'Do you mind if I have a look inside it?'; and an R would simply cut to the chase and say, 'What are the sales like?' or 'What are you doing on the PR front to help promote it?'

So use READ to help you *tailor* your message accordingly.

And, if you're giving a presentation to a group, you may want to consider using a blend of all four. Make your message clear and concise (to appeal to Rs), creative and engaging (to appeal to As), have a supplementary pack with loads of additional information (to appeal to Ds), and fortunately Es will probably like you and your talk, whatever you do.

Finally, just one more thought: whatever your personal READ profile might be, please be aware that there's no right one, or wrong one. They *all* have pluses and minuses in the workplace. Often it's a question of degree.

→ Rs, for example, are great at being direct (but sometimes they can be too direct).

→ Es are wonderfully nice (but sometimes they can be so nice that others take advantage of them).

→ As can be highly creative (but sometimes this can cause them to be chaotic).

→ Ds can be brilliant with detail (but sometimes they can become over-detailed, leading to death by PowerPoint or perhaps picky fault-finding).

Anyway, that's quite enough detail for now. The only reason for saying all this is to highlight how important it is to be able to *flex* your communication style, as and when necessary.

2 ALWAYS COMMUNICATE BENEFITS

One of the golden rules of business is that people seldom buy features, they buy benefits.

In other words, they're probably not that interested in the Black & Decker drill itself; they're more interested in the holes that the Black & Decker drill can help them create. Likewise, if they buy a Teflon saucepan, they're probably not that interested in the science of saucepans; they're more interested in how a Teflon saucepan can help them to cook without burning the food they're cooking.

With this in mind, as 'Everyone lives by selling something' (to quote the **Genius** Robert Louis Stevenson) here's a trick that can help you to turn the features of what you're selling into benefits, instantly.

It's basically three words that McDonald and Leppard recommend in their book *How to Sell a Service*, and those three words are: '*which means that ...*' So, for example, instead of saying, 'This jumper has a zip down the middle,' better to say, 'This jumper has a zip down the middle *which means that* you can take it off quickly, and easily, the moment you get hot, without having to pull it over your head'.

3 SHARPEN YOUR MESSAGE

A few years ago, when I travelled to Berlin to give a talk on innovation at a marketing conference, I had the opportunity to listen to one of the other speakers (whose message has always stuck with me).

He basically gave lots of green, blue, red and yellow balls to lots of different people in the audience and said: 'When I say go, please can you throw them at me all at once, and I'll try to catch them.' Sure enough, he couldn't. There were too many. And when he went to catch a new one, he ended up dropping an existing one.

Then, however, he deliberately gave *one ball* to *one person* in the audience, and asked them to throw it. This time he caught it easily. His point? People can't take in too much information, or too many messages, at one time. So, whatever message you want to communicate (unless you get paid to obfuscate) *keep it clear and simple* ...

BUSINESS GENIUS IN ACTION: NEXT STEPS ...

In summary, if you want to **UP!** your communication skills, here's how:

❶ Pinpoint the gap between *broadcasting* and *tailoring* (because effective communication isn't just a one-way street where we simply tell others what we want to say; it's more of a two-way exchange in which the message sent needs to be clearly understood by the receiver).

❷ Investigate how **Genius** communicators often *repackage* messages (for – as we saw with Visa, the Flying Scotsman, *Freakonomics* and David Ogilvy – it's not only *what* is said, but *how* it is said that matters).

❸ Leverage the power of READ (to help your business communications resonate with results-orientated people, emotions-orientated people, abracadabra-orientated people and data-orientated people).

❹ **O**rchestrate a plan to *sharpen* your communication (like the one ball, one message Berlin example I gave earlier, because this will enable you to break free from pointless information overload).

❺ **T**arget the amazing *benefits* of what you're selling (for at the end of the day people don't buy features, they buy benefits, so always use the three magic words of '*which means that ...*' to transform one into the other, instantly).

UP!SPIRATION
'Genius is the ability to put into effect what is on your mind.'
F. Scott Fitzgerald (author of *The Great Gatsby*)

UP! YOUR NEGOTIATION SKILLS

The tenth **B**lock and **L**imitation to **Business Genius** is **naive negotiating**.

And there are three main reasons for this:

→ Firstly, people naively assume they're much better at negotiating than they are …

(so they fall into the trap of *thinking on their feet*, when it would have been far wiser to plan ahead).

→ Secondly, people naively assume it's smart to go straight for the specifics of a deal such as 'how much?' and 'when by?' …

(so they fall into the trap of *depersonalising* the whole process, when it would have been far wiser to find common ground first).

→ Thirdly, people naively assume the only way to negotiate is to play hardball …

(so they fall into the trap of turning every negotiation into a *battle* with a winner and a loser, when often it would be wiser to work in partnership with others to move towards a mutually beneficial outcome).

Ultimately, the key to **Genius** negotiating is do the complete opposite, and to plan, personalise and partner!

In a moment we'll explore how.

Right now, however, there's one critical point we need to mention:

Negotiating isn't just one part of business: it *is* business

That's why in Roman times the word *negotiari* meant 'business', because the marketplace was all about 'settling or dealing by bargaining'.

And, by the way, just in case you think you're not the negotiating type – because you're not a high-flying lawyer, a highly committed Trade Union representative, or a highly influential rock 'n' roll manager like Colonel Tom Parker (who secured a deal in the 1950s that turned Elvis into the highest paid entertainer in the world at the age of 22) – please think again.

Negotiating is something we all do, most of the time, for, as the **Genius** actor Meryl Streep once said, raising a family is just one great 'enormous negotiation!'

OK, now we've got that out the way, let's focus on the art of negotiation itself. Please bear in mind, however, that what we're looking at here is principled negotiating, or what Leigh Steinberg – author of *Winning With Integrity: Getting what you're worth without selling your soul* – calls 'non-confrontational negotiating'.

(Obviously, in some parts of the world, where negotiating involves saying things like, 'We can't guarantee your safety if you don't sign on the dotted line' or 'Nice restaurant you've got here. Maybe you want to keep it that way?', it's a totally different story.)

Anyway, if it's a win-win you're after, here's a deceptively simple framework that can help. Before you enter into any negotiation, make sure you've already worked out your answers to these four questions:

❶ What would be a *fantastic* outcome?
(i.e. in an ideal world, what would you most love to walk away with?)

❷ What is the most *feasible* outcome?
(i.e. in the cool light of day, what do you think is most likely to happen?)

❸ What would be a *fundamental* outcome?
(i.e. how low are you fundamentally prepared to go?); and finally

❹ What is your *FOGG?*
(this one's a bit odd, but simply refers to Phileas Fogg – the
intrepid adventurer in Jules Verne's 1873 classic *Around the
World in Eighty Days* – because, in the heat of the moment
(if you're about to say yes to a deal that's even worse than
your fundamental position), how are you going to *escape* in
your equivalent of a hot-air balloon?)

Harvard negotiation experts Roger Fisher and William Ury
– authors of *Getting To Yes* – call this last one your 'best
alternative to a negotiated agreement' and, to be honest, it
can involve anything from 'buying time' (e.g. 'I need to consult
my boss on this before making a final decision') to perhaps
even walking away (especially if there are other business
opportunities you've already started to explore).

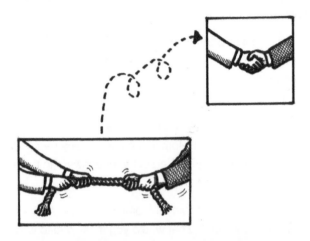

UP! YOUR NEGOTIATION SKILLS NUGGET

One of the most successful Asian businessmen of recent
times is Hong Kong's Li Ka-shing (otherwise known as the
'Warren Buffet of the East').

As business author Anthony Scaramucci makes clear in his book *Goodbye Gordon Gekko: How to find your fortune without losing your soul*, however, Li Ka-shing's success might never have happened if it hadn't have been for his **Genius** negotiation skills.

This is best summed up in the advice Li Ka-shing once gave Scaramucci:

> **'Leave money on the table for your partners. Not only will you be very rich, you will be very happy. If you allow your partners to benefit from the deal, they always come back and want to do business with you. There will never be a shortage of opportunity.'**

So, if you want to **UP!** your negotiation skills, please be mindful of how there's often a lot more to **Genius** negotiating than squeezing 'for the last nickel', time and time again.

Similarly, as Scaramucci writes, it's important to remember that capital is not only about 'cash, stocks and real estate': it's also about things like human capital, too, whereby (to be long-term **Business Geniuses**) we need to trust that our actions with others are 'worthwhile no matter what the return' might be.

Li Ka-shing

If you want to **UP!** your negotiation skills, here are three practical tips and strategies that may help:

1 PICTURE NEGOTIATING POSITIVELY

For years now, when I've run advanced negotiation skills programmes, I've invited small groups of people to picture what they think negotiation looks like. And the variety is often striking.

Some picture, for example, a tug of war (as I pictured earlier). Others see it as a game of chess (like a strategic mind game); a game of cards like poker (where it's all about bluff and double-bluff); or a dance (where 'it takes two to tango') or a sport (where there needs to be a 'level playing field').

The point being, often how we 'see' negotiation will influence how we go about negotiating.

So, if you're keen to excel in this area, choose imagery that helps you rather than scares you away.

After all, why can't mental pictures of negotiation be collaborative, rather than competitive, like a bridge, a rainbow, or a voyage of discovery?

And, if the last suggestion sounds a bit twee, here's a thought:

Chris Voss – an ex-FBI specialist in hostage negotiations – states: 'A negotiation is really a discovery process for both sides. That's one of the reasons that really smart people have trouble being negotiators – they're so smart they don't think they have anything to discover.'

2 REMEMBER EACH 'WAYNE'

Why is it that the young actor Marion Morrison had absolutely no say in his name being changed to John Wayne back in 1930? Well, back then, the legendary cowboy was simply a prop boy working with Fox Studios and, in the eyes of the movie director Raoul Walsh and studio head Winfield Sheehan, there were plenty of other aspiring actors who'd have jumped at the chance of being in the movie *The Big Trail* if he kicked up a fuss. In other words, *they* called the shots!

Compare and contrast this, however, with a very different Wayne (i.e. the England football striker Wayne Rooney). Why is it that his agent was able to secure him a new £300,000 a week deal with Manchester United in early 2014? Well, because Rooney was in such hot demand as a top goal scorer, there was no shortage of other teams queuing up to poach him, so Manchester United had little choice but to give him what he wanted. In other words, *he* called the shots!

Now, on the face of it, you may well be thinking, so what? Of course it's easier to negotiate when you're in a strong position, with plenty of leverage.

The key purpose of sharing the two Waynes example with you, however, wasn't that.

It was simply to show how *both* John Wayne *and* Wayne Rooney ended up walking away with good deals (as did Fox and Manchester United), in spite of them experiencing totally different types of negotiations.

In other words, had John Wayne insisted on clinging on to the name Marion Morrison, or said no to the lead role in *The Big Trail* (unless they changed it back again), would he have gone on to become such a silver-screen idol, and to star in 170 movies? Don't think so.

So, please remember this within the context of your own business negotiations. Sometimes (though not always) it can pay to lose a little, to gain a lot, further down the line …

3 MAKE, DON'T WIN

Finally, according to Tim Hindle in his book *Negotiating Skills*, it's important to recognise that 'a deal is made, not won'.

Or, to put it another way, as Brian Finch writes in *30 Minutes … To Negotiate a Better Deal*, 'The question "Who won?" is a meaningless one. If you achieved your objectives then you won, and why should you care if the other person won, too?'

BUSINESS GENIUS IN ACTION: NEXT STEPS …

In summary, if you want to **UP!** your negotiation skills, here's how:

❶ **P**inpoint why it's so important to plan, personalise and partner (to avoid falling into the traps of thinking on your feet, zooming straight ahead to dissect the data and playing hardball in every situation).

❷ **I**nvestigate how negotiating is something we all do, day in, day out (for this can help us to picture business negotiations more positively rather than *assuming* that only a small handful of people can do it, or do it well).

❸ **L**everage the power of principled negotiating (because it's often possible to get what you want without losing your soul).

④ **O**rchestrate a plan for using the four Fs (for the clearer you can be about what *fantastic, feasible, fundamental* and *FOGG* mean to you – in advance – the easier you'll find it to walk away with the deal you want).

⑤ **T**arget making a deal (recalling Brian Finch's advice that 'a deal is made, not won').

And remember movies and football and the two Waynes!

UP!SPIRATION
'In business, as in life, you don't get what you deserve, you get what you negotiate.'
Chester L. Karrass (author of *The Negotiating Game*)

PART 3
ACHIEVE IN BUSINESS

'Good is the enemy of great.'
Jim Collins

UP! YOUR COMPETITIVE ADVANTAGE

The eleventh **B**lock and **L**imitation to **Business Genius** is **invisible competitive advantage**.

Or, to put it another way, having a unique selling proposition (USP) that's incredibly hard for others to see.

If we want to excel in this area, it's vital we:

→ make it *easy* for others to *recognise* what makes our business offering different;

→ make it *easy* for others to *recognise* what a difference that difference can make to them!

Take Inspector Morse, for example.

Back in the early 1980s – according to the *American Spectator* journalist Larry Thornberry – TV cop shows like *Miami Vice* and *Hill Street Blues* were full of fast cars and blaring rock music.

But then along came *Morse* (based on the novels by Colin Dexter, and starring the actor John Thaw) which offered something 'refreshingly different from the usual cop show'.

Morse wasn't your average police inspector. Far from it. He was a 'cerebral, middle-aged, somewhat grumpy intellectual snob', who had studied Classics at Oxford, and had a passion for poetry and opera.

And, thanks to this *point of difference* – together with the show's serene soundtrack – Morse went on to become *instantly recognisable* around the world, not least in the UK where it was routinely watched by 15 million people!

So you may want to consider this, if you're aiming to **UP!** your competitive advantage.

Inspector Morse didn't only have something uniquely special about it; it also had something special that viewers valued, and didn't have to search too hard to find.

Morse, however, is just the tip of a massive iceberg.

All kinds of businesses over the years have found **Genius** ways of differentiating themselves from their rivals, in order to gain an **edge** …

Carl Fabergé, for example, (who became the official artist-jeweller to the Russian Tsar in 1885) gained his edge through exceptional craftsmanship and quality, and his distinctive Fabergé eggs are now universally recognised across the globe.

By contrast, Sam Walton – the **Business Genius** founder of Wal-Mart (the largest retailer in the world) – gained his edge by developing a dynamic 'low price, stack it high, and let it fly' retail strategy.

Fortunately, with a little imagination, the world's your oyster – as they say – when it comes to creating and sustaining superior performance.

Georgio Armani, for example, gained his edge by providing exceptional design, *Singapore Airlines* by providing exceptional customer service, *Dolby* and *Stradivari* by providing exceptional sound quality, and *Bloomberg* by providing exceptionally fast and reliable business news. And so the list goes on from the *Financial Times*' distinctive pink pages to Dyson's bagless vacuum cleaner.

Fundamentally, however, the underlying principle is the same. The key to competitive advantage is making sure your business 'Never copies mediocrity!' and continually asks the question, 'How can we do things differently to make things better around here?'

Or, as the marketing **Genius** Philip Kotler illuminates, it's built upon you being able to do something others 'cannot or will not match'.

And, finally, here's one bonus ladder of thought.

Michael E. Porter – the Harvard academic who's best known for his theories on the five forces of competitive advantage – managed to gain his edge from turning himself into the world's leading expert on … competitive advantage! Now that's **Business Genius!**

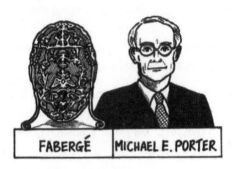

FABERGÉ   MICHAEL E. PORTER

UP! YOUR COMPETITIVE ADVANTAGE NUGGET

In the early 1900s, Coca-Cola – founded by the chemist Dr John Stith Pemberton (in Atlanta, 1886) – faced a serious commercial challenge.

The lucrative 'little tonic syrup mixed with water and baking soda' was in danger of being imitated, despite the large amounts of money it was spending on marketing and advertising.

This obviously meant it needed something else to boost its competitive advantage, and quickly, in order to still stand out from the crowd.

So what did Coca-Cola do?

Well, it leveraged the design **Genius** of Earl R. Dean (who worked for the Root Glass Company) who helped them come up with a radically new type of bottle. A bottle with unique contours inspired by the shape of the cocoa pod.

Consequently, ever since it first appeared in 1916, Coke's iconic bottle remains instantly recognisable the world over.

In fact, in early 2014 (almost 100 years later) Coca-Cola ingeniously decided to take this classic idea one step further.

It started to use the same design for its large 2-litre plastic bottles, too, together with the edgy strapline: 'Happiness is in a new bottle.'

So, maybe ask yourself how you could potentially design a better way forwards in the work that you do.

USEFUL TIPS AND ESCAPE STRATEGIES

If you want to **UP!** your competitive advantage, here are three practical tips and strategies that can help. Please note, however, that when we're talking about competitive advantage here, it doesn't solely have to apply to the private sector (i.e. to those selling financial services, snazzy clothes, or fizzy drinks).

On the contrary.

The concept that *better never stops* is becoming increasingly important in the public sector, too (e.g. for councils wanting to provide higher quality services than other councils, and for schools and colleges wishing to be more appealing to students than other schools and colleges, etc.).

Anyway, whatever it is you do for a living, please link the key messages back to your own unique situation.

1 OUT-THINK TO OUT-SMART

In the fiercely competitive world of modern business, it's vital we keep our thinking as sharp as possible.

Or, as Michael Bergdahl emphasises in his book *What I Learned from Sam Walton: How to compete and thrive in a Wal-Mart world*, 'If you want to avoid being crushed by your competition you have to out-think, out-plan, out-work, and out-execute, 52 weeks a year.'

Woolworths, for example, used to have an edge in business for many years (as did HMV, Blockbuster, Golden Wonder Crisps and Clinton Cards). But, having an edge, and retaining an edge, are not the same thing!

So to prevent **strategic drift** from happening to you, I'd strongly recommend two pieces of valuable advice (the first from the innovation expert Roger von Oech, and the second from the *Mavericks at Work* authors William C. Taylor and Polly Labarre):

❶ Bear in mind it's not always enough to go for the right answer in business. Sometimes we need to go for the second right answer, or the third right answer, because that way we'll be far less predictable.

❷ Bear in mind it's not always enough to look at best practice in business, because that'll only tell us what our competitors are doing right now.

Far better to also look at next practice, so you and your business don't get left behind.

2 GO FOR INNOVATIVENESS

One of the most common mistakes businesses make with competitive advantage is they focus too much on innovation and not enough on innovativeness.

Yes, of course, they overlap, but they're not the same thing.

According to Mark O'Hare in his 1988 book *Innovate! How to Gain and Sustain Competitive Advantage*, he writes how 'innovations can take a company forwards' but 'innovativeness can take it much further'.

If we spend all our time developing the new X17 gadget, for example, it's very possible someone else will come along with an even better X17+, X18 or X19, before the paint's had time to dry.

After all, look at what happened to BlackBerry. According to David Robertson (writing in *The Times* in March 2012): 'For many years, BlackBerry dominated the smartphone market but the arrival of the iPhone and other devices with web browsing and media applications caused BlackBerry's market share to fall by 75 per cent, and its profits to fall by two-thirds, in a single year.'

Developing innovativeness, therefore, is arguably the wiser strategy (e.g. by helping employees build their creativity capacity by attending regular lateral thinking training programmes, or by reading books like W. Chan Kim and Renée Mauborgne's *Blue Ocean Strategy* to help expand their minds). That way, a business will be better placed to come up with innovation, after innovation, after innovation …

Innovativeness appears to hold the key to what O'Hare calls 'defensible competitive advantage', because 'without this, innovation is tactical, not strategic'.

3 FLY LIKE THUNDERBIRDS

Back in the 1960s the **Genius** Gerry Anderson created a highly successful TV phenomenon known as *Thunderbirds*.

It used a special technique called supermarionation, involving puppets suspended by thin metal wires, whose mouths moved up and down using remote controls to create the illusion they were speaking.

Anyway, the point is, it was different and, if you want to gain competitive advantage in business, it's *difference* not *blandness* that will help you achieve it.

After all, that's how Arthur Baldwin Turnure gained an edge in 1892 when he founded a very different type of magazine (*Vogue*), and Pierre Omidyar gained an edge in 1997 when he provided a very different way of auctioning online (eBay).

BUSINESS GENIUS IN ACTION: NEXT STEPS ...

In summary, if you want to **UP!** your competitive advantage, here's how:

❶ Pinpoint to what extent your competitive advantage is clearly visible (because if your business offering looks much the same everyone else's – in the eyes of potential competitors – you could end up as transparent as H. G. Wells's 1897 creation, *The Invisible Man*).

② Investigate how others have succeeded in developing a USP (as we did earlier with *Inspector Morse*, Fabergé, the *Financial Times* and Earl R. Dean's iconic Coca-Cola bottle, because exploring the successes of others can often inspire us to forge our own).

③ Leverage the power of innovativeness (because – as Mark O'Hare points out – focusing on innovation alone is seldom more than tactical).

④ Orchestrate a plan to look at next practice, not just best practice (to help you avoid strategic drift, and being left behind in a fast-changing world).

⑤ Target being different (however – like *Thunderbirds*, *Vogue* and eBay – just make sure what makes you different is genuinely valued by others).

UP!SPIRATION
'The only sustainable competitive advantage is an organisation's ability to learn faster than the competition.'
Peter M. Senge (senior lecturer, MIT)

UP! YOUR BUSINESS GROWTH

The twelfth **B**lock and **L**imitation to **Business Genius** is **insufficient business growth**.

And the reason for this is simple.

Business (like life itself) won't stand still and so, if we're not 'progressing all the time' – as Sir John Harvey-Jones (the former Chairman of ICI) used to say – we are in fact 'just going backwards'.

Now, of course, if you're lucky there's always the slim possibility you may be able to grow your business without growing your business. Pencil sales in the UK, for example, rose by over 400 per cent in the early 2000s, because Sudoku suddenly became popular. Likewise, enlistment in the US Airforce rocketed by over 500 per cent in 1986, thanks to Tony Scott and Jerry Bruckheimer's super-cool 'I feel the need for speed' movie *Top Gun*, which made flying jets sexier and wilder than ever! But relying on this type of 'luck' is not the wisest strategy.

Far better to drive growth actively, rather than passively because, as B. C. Forbes (founder of *Forbes Magazine*, 1880– 1954) exclaimed: 'If you don't drive your business, you will be driven out of business.'

So, with this in mind, if you're keen to help your business growth soar like an Andean condor (whether that means growth in terms of profit, productivity, people development or public services delivery), here's a model I developed that is designed to help, inspired by a business friend of mine called Roy Sheppard.

To cut to the chase, it's based on the idea that there are only really four ways to grow a business – whatever that business might be – and those four ways are: Spotting, Opening up, Attracting and Raising (hence the acronym SOAR). And here's how it works.

SPOTTING

The first way to grow your business involves spotting customers you may not have noticed before. That's to say, it's like looking through a massive telescope at a massive universe to explore who else is out there.

India, for example, is famous for its tea drinking, yet in September 2005 Costa Coffee suddenly spotted the commercial potential of becoming the 'first international coffee chain' to enter into this new market.

Similarly, before 1980, the cosmetics company Nivea focused on providing skincare products for women, but then they spotted how skincare products aimed at men could be hugely lucrative, too.

How about we go back even further to 1919? That's when the yogurt company Danone (set up by Isaac Carasso in Barcelona) was essentially a health food business that sold through pharmacies to help young children suffering from intestinal disorders after the First World War. It was Carasso's son Daniel, however (after whom the business was named), who spotted how the business could be much more than that, and so he helped grow it by making the yogurts more tasty to attract a broader range of customers and soon Danone started distributing through dairy-food shops as well.

OPENING UP

The second way to grow your business is to open up (i.e. diversify and explore what else the business could potentially move into).

When Charles Henry Harrod (1799–1885), for example, set up shop in 1849, he mainly sold tea and groceries in a single room with two assistants and a messenger boy. Step-by-step, however, Harrods steadily opened up into the world-famous department store we know today (spread over 7 floors, 15 million visitors a year and worth over £1.5 billion!), which prides itself on being able to sell 'All things for all people' from shoes to perfume to garden furniture.

Likewise, according to Allyn Freeman in his book *The Leadership Genius of Alfred P. Sloan*, when Sloan took over General Motors back in the 1920s, his approach to business growth was far more open than Henry Ford's, who famously exclaimed: 'You can have it in any colour, as long as it's black.'

Sloan's innovative leadership focused on a 'car for every price and purpose offering'. Consequently, between 1923 and 1936, Ford's market share fell from 60 per cent to 22 per cent, whilst General Motor's rose to 43 per cent!

ATTRACT

The third way to grow your business is to keep attracting people back, so they end up buying from you, again and again (i.e. exploring how else you can drum up repeat business).

That's why we have everything from loyalty cards to Gillette throw-away razors, and printer cartridges to lightbulbs (that constantly need replacing). It's also why the cereal manufacturer of Shredded Wheat managed to boost its sales in 1982 with its ingenious 'Bet you can't eat three' campaign, which had children all over the country wolfing down cereal to prove they could (and finishing the packets more speedily in the process).

RAISE

The fourth and final way to grow your business is to keep raising the value (or perceived value) of your business offering, so you can start to charge more for your products or services.

Doctors, for example, can raise the value of their business by specialising in a specific area (like training to become a cardiologist, an obstetrician, or a brain surgeon); business schools, can raise the value of their institutions by securing prestigious MBA accreditations; and owners of restaurants can raise the value of their business by winning awards (like the 36-year-old culinary **Genius** René Redzepi whose restaurant Noma, in Denmark, not only recently received its second Michelin Star, but also received its Best Restaurant in the World award for the fourth year running!).

One of the most extraordinary examples of raise in action, however, has got to be that of the diamond company De Beers. Admittedly, it's hard to believe now, but back in the 1930s the global demand for diamonds was in a nosedive, and so De Beers realised they needed a cunningly clever plan to reverse their fortunes. So what did they do?

Well, with the help of the New York ad agency N. W. Ayer & Son, they came up with the ingenious idea of wedding diamonds with romance (in the eyes and minds of the public), and launched a massive publicity campaign featuring Hollywood stars and royalty to promote this message.

As a result, 'The Diamond Invention' (as American journalist E. J. Epstein calls it) was born!

Almost overnight, as they say, diamond engagement rings (which hadn't taken off before, because many preferred coloured stones) started to become the 'only' type of engagement rings worth having. But here was the real **Genius** bit. As Epstein explains, for men a diamond engagement ring started to be viewed as a gift of love, and for women it started to be viewed as a part of courtship. Consequently, it wasn't only that more people started to buy more diamonds, they also started to buy more expensive diamonds! As a result, data suggests that, in 1939, 'annual sales of the gem were around

$23 million', yet by 1979 – largely thanks to this ingenious campaign – sales had 'expanded to $2.1 billion'.

No wonder the strapline 'A diamond is forever' (created by the **Genius** copywriter Frances Gerety in 1948) is still going strong today.

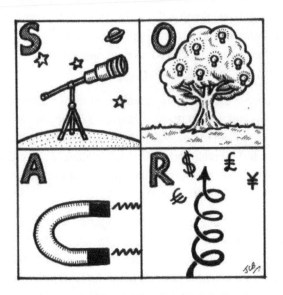

UP! YOUR BUSINESS GROWTH NUGGET

Up until the 1950s, most toy dolls around the world either looked like babies, or they looked like young girls.

That's how it was.

But then along came a **Business Genius** called Ruth Handler, who turned this on its head.

Inspired by her visit to Germany in 1956, Handler mused over what might happen if toy dolls looked like grown-ups instead, so that young girls could play with them, dress them up, and feel 'grown up' doing so.

And from that *seed* of an idea, Mattel launched the first Barbie doll in 1959 and, since then, the stats on its growth have been astronomical!

According to John Haydon – writing in *The Washington Times* in April 2012 – for example, it's estimated that 300,000 Barbies were sold in 1959 alone, but over the last 50 years they've gone on to sell *billions*.

In fact, other sources (like www.barbiemedia.com) state that 'One Barbie doll is sold every three seconds somewhere in the world' and '90 per cent of girls [between the ages of 3 and 10] own at least one Barbie doll.'

Not only that, however, in terms of SOAR, it appears that Barbie sales have been boosted in all four ways! Spotting (has enabled Barbie to be sold in 150 different countries), Opening up (has enabled Barbie to diversify into films and music), Attract (has been achieved through the selling of endless clothing and furniture accessories), and Raise (has been achieved by providing premium value dolls produced as limited editions). **Genius!**

If you want to **UP!** your business growth, here are three practical tips and strategies that can help:

1 KEEP ON LEARNING

It's said that lobsters never stop growing, which may be one of the reasons they live to over 150 years old!

People, however, are very different to lobsters.

We often do stop growing – in the educational sense – and we stop growing because we stop learning.

So, if you want yourself, your colleagues and your business to keep surviving and thriving in a highly competitive world, please remember to keep 'Filling the well' (as creativity expert Julia Cameron recommends) with plenty of new ideas and fresh perspectives, so the well never runs dry.

Please note, however, that learning doesn't always have to involve 'content-increasing' knowledge (i.e. filling our heads with more and more data).

Often, as Robert T. Kiyosaki, the author of *Rich Dad, Poor Dad*, illuminates: 'Context-expanding knowledge can be just as important for growth, if not more so, because it can enable us to look at what we do know through a slightly different lens.'

Admittedly, not everyone accepts the view that learning is important (even though there is a wise Chinese proverb that states 'Learning is a treasure that will follow its owner everywhere') but, in terms of your personal career plan, here's some smart advice from Reid Hoffman (the co-founder of LinkedIn) who states: 'You have to be constantly reinventing yourself and investing in your future …'

2 EXPECT THE UNEXPECTED

Evidence suggests that business growth can take years to build, but occasionally plummet in an instant.

Look at the French beret business, for example. For years and years berets sold well in France, but then in 2001 the unexpected happened. The French Government introduced a new piece of legislation, which ended military conscription, and suddenly the demand for 400,000 extra army berets each year vanished into thin air!

So, if you want your business growth to stay healthy, it can be beneficial to use things like *scenario planning* – which Shell made famous back in the 1970s – to help think the unthinkable, imagine the unimaginable, and prepare for both.

3 CREATE NEW CURVES

Forgive me if you've come across the Sigmoid Curve before. The only reason I'm mentioning it, however, is because it would be a bit bonkers to write about business growth without doing so. Anyway, I'll do my best to keep it short.

Back in the 1990s – in Charles Handy's book *The Age of Unreason* – Handy emphasised how, 'What gets you to where you are,' in business, 'won't always keep you where you are.' And, within that context, he wrote about something called the Sigmoid Curve, which basically looks like the letter 'S' that's fallen flat on its face. Rather like this …

What does it mean? Well, if you imagine performance running along the vertical axis, and time running along the horizontal axis, it means that more or less everything in life – from the Roman Empire, to a relationship, a business, and even life itself – inevitably follows this predictable pattern. To begin with, performance dips (because we make mistakes as we learn the ropes) then performance steadily improves, until everything – over time – starts to wax and wane.

Handy's key message, however, was that if we leave growth and innovation to the end of the curve (point B), we've probably left it too late! Far better to start moving on to the next big thing at point A (i.e. before we need to), and that way we'll be able to keep growing and staying forever fresh and relevant (as you can see in the picture below).

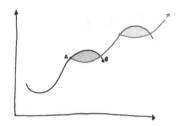

BUSINESS GENIUS IN ACTION: NEXT STEPS ...

In summary, if you want to **UP!** your business growth, here's how:

❶ Pinpoint what business growth ultimately means to you (because, as Tony Robbins states: 'As is the gardener, so is the garden').

② Investigate how growth is no longer an option, it's a necessity (for – as Sir John Harvey-Jones remarked – 'If we're not progressing all the time we are in fact just going backwards').

③ Leverage the power of SOAR (as everyone from Costa Coffee to Nivea, and Danone to Barbie have done over the years. In other words, turn to Spotting, Opening up, Attracting and Raising whenever you need help growing from where you are, to where you want to be).

④ Orchestrate a plan to keep 'Filling the well' (for businesses need a constant supply of fresh ideas and fresh learning, to stay … fresh !).

⑤ Target new curves (by constantly remembering Charles Handy's advice that 'What gets you to where you are won't keep you where you are').

UP!SPIRATION
'You can't shrink your way to greatness.'
Tom Peters (management expert and co-author of *In Search of Excellence*)

UP! YOUR INNOVATION CULTURE

The thirteenth **B**lock and **L**imitation to **Business Genius** is a **stifling organisational culture**.

In other words, a culture where there's very little wriggle room to think differently, let alone do things differently.

And what causes this? Bureaucracy? Office politics? Protocol?

Well, according to Harvard academic Teresa Amabile, it basically boils down to four things: too much *surveillance*, too much *control*, too much *evaluation*, and too many *relentless deadlines*.

By contrast, in the eyes of business author Robert Hartley, it boils down to three things: *complacency* (e.g. 'We don't need to change, because we're fine as we are'), *conceit* (e.g. 'We don't need to change, because we're better than everyone else') and *conservatism* (e.g. 'We don't need to change because the old ways are the best').

But let's boil it down even further. Let's boil it down to *one* thing.

'You can't do that here!'

Yes, I know it sounds crazily simple, but this *one* sentence ultimately sums up what a stifling culture is all about.

And here's why.

According to innovation expert Jonne Ceserani – in his book *Big Ideas: Putting the zest into creativity and innovation at work* – there's far more to this sentence than meets the eye because, depending on how one says it, it can mean five very different things:

'*You* can't do that here!', for example, might well mean '*I* can do it, but *you* can't (because I'm more powerful than you are),' so the stifling issue in a business like this would be linked to structures, hierarchy and identity.

'You *can't* do that here!' would be linked to beliefs and attitudes.

'You can't *do* that here!' would be linked to capability and skills.

'You can't do *that* here!' would be linked to behaviour.

And 'You can't do that *here*!' would be linked to the environment.

And this is why it's no coincidence that **Business Genius** moments are far more likely to flourish in a **can-do culture** where there's plenty of *permission* to experiment, explore and excite – such as Pixar, Virgin, 3M, Innocent and Ben & Jerry's ice cream – than in a **you can't do that here! culture**, where there isn't.

This doesn't mean, however, that I'm suggesting you throw caution to the wind with your own business, and start to feel so *liberated* and *creative* that everything comes crashing down like a house of cards.

On the contrary.

I'm simply suggesting that a **no mistakes culture** (i.e. a culture where people can't even make excusable mistakes, never mind inexcusable mistakes) is unlikely to spark innovative thinking and innovative solutions.

Besides, as Professor Robert I. Sutton of Stanford points out: 'The best single question for testing an organisation's character is: "What happens when people make mistakes?"'

Finally, however, please consider this: many organisations look upon efficiency as the key to success (and, in many instances, this may be so).

In Paul Sloane's book *The Leader's Guide to Lateral Thinking Skills*, however, he convincingly argues that **innovation** invariably beats efficiency time and time again because you could carry on making more and more efficient horse-drawn carriages (but then along comes the automobile), more and more efficient gaslights (but then along comes the electric light), or more and more efficient typewriters (but then along come electronic word processors).

Thinking better often matters in business. Yet thinking differently often matters more ...

UP! YOUR INNOVATION CULTURE NUGGET

When the Brazilian businessman Ricardo Semler took over his father's business in 1981, he wasn't that interested in doing things differently; he wanted to do things *totally* differently!

As a result, the industrial equipment manufacturer he inherited (called Semco) soon developed into one of the most innovative organisational cultures on the planet:

→ 'Workers made the decisions previously made by their bosses.'

→ 'Managerial staff set their own salaries and bonuses ... without strings.'

→ 'Everyone was given access to the company books.'

→ 'Shop floor workers set their own productivity targets and schedules.'

Now, I'm not suggesting every company does a Semco. Far from it.

The reason I'm including this nugget is simply to highlight how – if business success is anything to go by – Semler's approach wasn't perhaps as crazy as it seemed.

In Semler's book *Maverick!: The success story behind the world's most unusual workplace*, for example (which was first published in 1993) his unorthodox approach went on to help the business grow eleven-fold, which was incredible, bearing in mind that inflation in Brazil back then was running at 900 per cent!

Not only this, however; it meant that they had 2,000 people on their waiting list who were longing to join, including hundreds who said they would take any job just to work there.

So what was the innovative idea behind all this? Well, Semler writes how it was simply 'To make people look forward to coming to work in the morning ...' and, let's face it, any business leader who can achieve that with their employees has to be a **Genius!**

RICARDO SEMLER

So, if you want to **UP!** your innovation culture, here are three practical tips and strategies that can help:

1 PROVIDE 'PSYCHOLOGICAL SAFETY'

Years ago, I was doing some consulting work for a large organisation in London when I walked past their spanking new, state-of-the-art creativity zone. It looked fantastic. Colourful beanbags, plenty of games and ideas stimulus, and it even had wacky ornaments dangling from the ceiling. 'Why is no one in there?' I asked. 'Oh,' I was told, 'you wouldn't be seen dead in there. People would think you're not working!'

This insight led me to develop what I call the **platinum rule of business innovation**, which is this:

People need to feel safe enough to *stop* playing it safe

Yes, it's a paradox, but the underlying principle is an important one.

Fear and creativity don't mix!

And the reason they don't mix – according to very clever people who walk around in white coats – is because they involve completely different brainwaves.

If someone is incredibly focused on something, for example (like sitting an exam, or meeting a deadline), brainwaves called Beta brainwaves kick in. These look a little like the short, jagged glass you might see on brick walls to deter burglars and, in terms of neuroscientific gobbledegook, their wave frequencies are between 14–40 Hz. By contrast, if that same person was fast asleep and totally relaxed, Delta brainwaves (i.e. less than 4 Hz) would emerge, which look a little like the large, rolling hills found in the Lake District.

The ones in between, however, (i.e. Alpha and Theta brainwaves, which are between 4 Hz and 14 Hz) are the ones most closely connected with creative thinking, as well as daydreaming and meditation, etc.

What this means is that we invariably come up with our best ideas when we're focused (but not over-focused) and relaxed (but not over-relaxed), which is why Dickens got his best ideas *going for a long walk*, J. K. Rowling from *sitting in a café*, Edward de Bono whilst *shaving*.

Here's the point, however.

If we work in a climate of fear (e.g. where we're permanently worried about what our boss will say, or whether we'll still have a job tomorrow) Beta brainwaves will naturally take over. And what does this mean? It means we go into emergency thinking, which means we focus on what works (because it's worked before), and this means … goodbye creativity!

2 NURTURE OTHERS' GENIUS

I recently asked a group – I was running a Lateral Thinking seminar – 'What's the one word that kills creativity more than anything else in business?' (expecting them to say 'But', or something like that). Someone, however, simply said, 'Manager!' I thought it was a joke, but it then transpired that their manager even had a nickname which was Dr No (because they were always saying 'No' to everything). Anyway, I'm not saying this to be unkind. I'm saying it because often a manager is not deliberately trying to crush the creativity of others; they've simply never been shown how *not* to kill it. So, with this in mind, here's an effective three-step process, which business trainer Julie Hay recommends, that can help:

❶ *Paraphrase.* So, if someone at work approaches you with *their* **Business Genius** idea of painting all the blue boxes red, simply feed back what you've heard, for example, say: 'So your idea is to paint the blue boxes red.' (This will demonstrate that you've been *listening*!).

❷ *Praise.* There is virtually always something positive (or potentially positive) about an idea, even though you might have to dig hard to find it. In this case, go on to say something like: 'That definitely sounds innovative, and it would help us to differentiate them from the yellow ones.'

❸ Here's the crucial bit, *position.* In other words, if the nagging thought at the back of your mind is, 'No way! We can't afford it!', instead of saying that – which will flatten their inventiveness – find a way to reposition the same message to avoid doing more harm than good. For example, say: 'Have you any ideas on where we might be able to find a budget for this?'

Using this approach often has two key benefits: on the one hand it encourages them to use their creativity to fix the potential problem, because they may be able to go away and find a budget for it, if they move a few things around; on the other, it means that they're more likely to come to you with their *next* **Business Genius** idea, which might end up being the real winner!

3 REVEL IN VARIETY

The culture of Renaissance Florence was, arguably, one of the most innovative cultures of all time. Why? Because in Renaissance times it was perfectly normal for people like

Leonardo Da Vinci to be polymaths (variety-seekers who were not only painters and sculptors, but also scientists, musicians and architects, etc.). If you want *your* culture to be more innovative, remember that innovation often evolves out of the rich *cross-fertilisation* of different people, from different departments, who have different perspectives and ideas.

BUSINESS GENIUS IN ACTION: NEXT STEPS ...

In summary, if you want to **UP!** your innovation culture, here's how:

❶ **P**inpoint effective ways to create wriggle room in your culture (because without it people's **Business Genius** will soon become stifled by an endless barrage of, 'You can't do that here!).

❸ **I**nvestigate how other businesses have managed to excel in this area (from Pixar to Virgin and 3M to Innocent, to spark your own innovative thinking and innovative behaviours).

❸ **L**everage the power of permission (remembering the platinum rule of business innovation: 'People need to feel safe enough to *stop* playing it safe').

❹ **O**rchestrate a plan for nurturing the **Business Genius** of others (for it could be that all the breakthrough ideas you're looking for are locked inside the minds of those you work with, just waiting to be released).

❺ **T**arget infinite variety (because – like the polymaths of Renaissance Florence – an innovation culture often stems from the rich cross-fertilisation of different perspectives and different ideas).

UP!SPIRATION
'Innovation = breaking today's rules.'
Steve Jobs (co-founder of Apple)

UP! YOUR
COLLABORATION

The fourteenth **B**lock and **L**imitation to **Business Genius** is **careless collaboration**.

And it's often careless for two main reasons:

❶ People are careless about *the way* they collaborate with others (which often leads to conflict).

❷ People couldn't care less about collaborating with others (which often leads to missed opportunities).

Let's take a closer look at the second.

It's hardly surprising – in the real world of work – that not everyone welcomes **collaboration** with open arms.

After all, collaborating with others can be extremely time-consuming (if you're constantly having to ask for everyone's opinion on everything), and it can also be extremely irritating (if others have a propensity to 'park their tanks on your lawn'!)

That aside, however, it doesn't take a **Genius** to realise that when collaboration does work well, the business benefits are often far greater than the sum of the parts.

Look at the business collaboration that first started in 1904, for example, when Henry Edmunds introduced two people to one another (at a Manchester hotel), thinking they might get on: one was an engineer called Henry Royce, and the other a businessman called Charles Rolls.

Or look of the business collaboration that first started in 1837 when a man called Alexander Norris floated the notion that the husband of one of his daughters (Olivia) might be better off working with the husband of his other daughter (Elizabeth). One was called William Procter (who made candles for a living), and the other was called James Gamble (who made bars of soap).

Effective collaborations can often spark moments of **Business Genius** that probably wouldn't have happened on a solo basis (from Elton John and Bernie Taupin to Marks & Spencer, and even the iconic Concorde).

Unfortunately, however, although 'many leaders inherently know that in today's competitive environment companywide collaboration is imperative for successful strategy execution' – as collaboration expert Morten Hansen observes – there's frequently a hairy old troll guarding the bridge: and that troll is office politics.

That's to say, what's good for a business might not always be perceived as good by the individuals in that business. Consequently, this can lead to all kinds of non-collaborative behaviours from important information not being shared, to traditionalists and progressives ending up at loggerheads with one another and, worst of all, trust breaking down.

With this in mind, if you want to **UP!** your collaboration and work jointly on an activity or project it's important to realise that collaboration is simply a **conflict management style**. Or, more specifically – as Kenneth Thomas and Ralph Kilmann pinpointed in 1974 (in their research tool, the Thomas-Kilmann Conflict Mode Instrument) – simply one of the five conflict management styles, which include:

❶ *Competing*: like boxers in a ring, where there's a winner and a loser.

❷ *Compromising*: where both parties win a bit, and lose a bit.

❸ *Accommodating*: where one person backs down to let the other win.

❹ *Avoiding*: where both parties ultimately end up losing.

❺ *Collaborating*: which is the all-too-familiar win–win scenario.

Although this might sound pretty obvious, however, here's something that's perhaps a little less obvious. In terms of the

Thomas-Kilmann model, collaboration turns out to be the complete opposite of avoiding. After all, ever tried to collaborate with someone who is as elusive as the Scarlet Pimpernel? That's why the secret of effective collaboration is **inclusivity** (i.e. drawing the pieces of the jigsaw closer together) rather than **exclusivity** (i.e. pushing them further apart) …

UP! YOUR COLLABORATION NUGGET

When the legendary rock band the Eagles wrote *Hotel California* back in 1976, it was a classic example of collaboration in action.

To begin with, it started out as a guitar riff created by Don Felder (who was evidently a great guitar player, but not much of a singer).

Then – using Felder's rough demo tape as a foundation for the song – fellow band members Don Henley and Glenn Frey began to embellish it.

But that wasn't the end of it.

As the songwriting and recording developed, the infamous long guitar solo at the end – featuring Felder and co-guitarist Joe Walsh – emerged out of the two desperately trying to outplay one another because of their intense rivalry. And this was a sign of things to come ...

The purpose of this nugget is simply to demonstrate how collaborating isn't always easy, and it isn't always painless, for, by 1980 – when the Eagles had become the biggest band in America – there were so many fights and hostile exchanges of words, they finally split up. More to the point, they were so angry with one another, they promised their fans they would only play again, 'When Hell freezes over!'

So, what happened?

Well, 14 years later they started to collaborate again and recorded another hit album called ... *Hell Freezes Over*. **Genius!**

USEFUL TIPS AND ESCAPE STRATEGIES

If you want to **UP!** your collaboration, here are three practical tips and strategies that can help:

1 PICTURE AN ORANGE

I once stumbled across an intriguing insight on conflict resolution by the US business consultant Bob Lapin.

Lapin told the story of two young boys (brothers, to be precise) who kept squabbling over an orange because they both wanted it, and there was only *one* available.

Eventually, having bickered and argued for so long, they ran up to their father to make the final decision on who should have it.

So what does he do?

Well, the standard answer is, 'Cut it in half!' (**compromise**). Perfectly logical; perfectly fair.

'No,' says Lapin. 'The father asks them *why* they want the orange.'

One says, 'Because Mummy says they're good for me and they're full of Vitamin C,' and the other says, 'Because I want to make Mummy an orange birthday cake.'

So the father ends up giving the fruit to one, and the peel to the other.

Anyway, the point of the story is – as you can no doubt tell – often in business it can be highly tempting to go straight for the compromise, but it's only when we *listen* and find out what the real issues are that we can make an informed decision.

2 WELCOME 'CREATIVE ABRASION'

This one's far from easy, because when people get on our nerves or wind us up at work, the prospect of collaborating with them is usually the last thing on our mind.

In psychology, however, there's a phenomenon called **creative abrasion**, which sheds light on how a little bit of friction and tension (in a group dynamic) is often no bad thing.

Or, to follow on from the Eagles example earlier: 'A bit of craziness,' as Eagle's guitarist Joe Walsh once said, can be useful for 'fanning the artistic fire'.

Please don't think, however, that creative abrasion has relevance only in the world of rock.

It is also relevant for virtually any business, or business team, because without creative abrasion there's always the danger of **groupthink.** Put simply, groupthink – a term the psychologist Irving Janis invented in the 1970s – occurs when people value consensus over and above the fixing of problems.

One of the most famous, and tragic, examples of this was when the NASA *Challenger* blew up. After the event, it turned out that many individuals working on the programme had *silent reservations* about some of the technical safety issues but, when they were in a group context, they kept these thoughts to themselves because they didn't want to be seen as troublemakers, or negative influences on such a positive and pioneering journey into space.

Within the context of your own collaborations you may want to reflect upon what thoughts are *not* being said, for pretending everything is hunky-dory (when it isn't) seldom helps anyone in the long-run.

3 VIEW COLLABORATION 'REALISTICALLY'

One of the great ironies of collaboration training programmes is that the people who come on them tend to be fairly collaborative anyway. It's the ones who stay away (either because they're too busy or because something's cropped up) that, arguably, need to be there the most.

That said, however: it's important we view collaboration **realistically** (rather than idealistically).

The bottom line is that we can't *make* other people collaborate (even if we'd like to). Of course we can have a good try – by using all the tools, techniques and insights under the sun – but, at the end of the day, if they don't want to collaborate, they won't. Far better that we focus on the difference *we* can make to *our* part of the collaborative process, because by osmosis that can help to change the overall dynamic.

Another part of viewing collaboration realistically, however, involves accepting that sometimes – if the co-operative spirit just isn't there – it could be time to shift direction. Back in the late 1940s, for example (in the German town of Herzogenaurach, Bavaria) two brothers weren't just bickering over an orange; they were finding it hard to collaborate on their joint business. So what happened? Well, Adolf Dassler set off to set up Adidas and, on the other side of the road, Rudolf Dassler set up Puma!

BUSINESS GENIUS IN ACTION: NEXT STEPS ...

In summary, if you want to **UP!** your collaboration, here's how:

❶ Pinpoint how collaboration is ultimately a conflict management style (and, like competing, compromising, being accomodating and avoiding, it can work well in some situations, yet less well in others).

❷ Investigate what an amazing difference collaboration can make (from Rolls-Royce to Procter & Gamble and Lennon and McCartney to Goscinny and Uderzo (the creators of Asterix). This, in turn, can then inspire you to develop dynamic business collaborations of your own, based on the principle that the whole is often greater than the sum of its parts).

❸ Leverage the power of inclusivity (because it's incredibly hard for collaboration to work well when people are as elusive as the Scarlet Pimpernel!).

❹ Orchestrate a plan to heal rifts (for, although it doesn't always work, the Eagles managed to do it when they finally reunited in 1994).

❺ Target oranges (or at least remember the story of the orange mentioned earlier, for it will help to remind you that racing ahead for a quick compromise may often be the easiest business option, but it's not always the wisest).

UP!SPIRATION

'If everyone is moving forward together then success takes care of itself.'

Henry Ford (founder of Ford Motor Company)

UP! YOUR LEADERSHIP SKILLS

The fifteenth **B**lock and **L**imitation to **Business Genius** is **uninspiring leadership**.

Now, admittedly, in days gone by – when the boss was the boss, others were ludicrously lucky to have a job, and that was the end of it – this didn't matter too much.

Nowadays, however, the inspirational dimension of leadership appears to matter more than ever, for as Deborah Meaden (of the enterprising TV show *The Dragon's Den*) highlights:

'A leader's job is to inspire!'

Unfortunately, however, **inspiring** (which basically means to breathe into) doesn't come naturally to many leaders, who may be technically brilliant, and financially astute, but far less skilled at securing commitment.

So what's the secret of 'bringing others with you', as Kevin Murray (author of *The Language of Leaders*) would say?

Well, in many ways, it is focusing as much on what you *don't do*, as what you *do*.

Inspiring leaders, for example, don't micro-manage, credit steal, crush creativity, talk defeat, dither with decision making, or alienate employees by behaving inauthentically.

On the contrary.

For as a leadership expert friend of mine Khoi Tu (author of *Superteams*) explains:

'Leaders can easily *lose* followers if they can't answer the following four questions:

Where are we now?

Where are we going?

Why are we going there?

How will we get there?'

In other words, it is the role of a leader to set direction, manage and develop talent and, perhaps most importantly, to create an environment for success!

Having said this, however, it is important to remember that even the most inspirational leaders in the world are not magicians or wizards (even though the halo effect might lead us to believe otherwise).

They can only help to bring out the best in the people they work with for, as Jim Collins writes in *Good to Great*: 'Great vision without great people is irrelevant.'

It is also important to remember, however, that **leadership** – which President Eisenhower defined as, 'getting others to do what you want because they want to do it' – doesn't apply only to the chief executives of gigantic organisations!

Far from it.

Because, as leadership specialist Fredrik Arnander makes clear:

'We are all leaders:
leadership is not a position it is a mindset'

And this is why we need to be aware that, even if we're not a formal leader in an organisation (who has responsibility and authority in role), we can still be a mindset leader (who takes responsibility and has authority in person).

UP! YOUR LEADERSHIP SKILLS
NUGGET

One of the most inspirational experts on leadership, over the past few decades, is Ken Blanchard (author of *The One Minute Manager* and *Leading at a Higher Level*).

Not only has he long championed the idea of catching people doing something right in the workplace, and then praising them straight away (rather than waiting for people to slip up, and then come down on them like a ton of bricks for doing so); perhaps, more importantly, he also co-pioneered the concept of **situational leadership**. It has been around for many years – so you may well have come across it before – however, here's a quick taster. Historically, it's often been assumed that you're either a leader or you're not. In the 1970s, however, Paul Hersey and Ken Blanchard challenged this view, based on the idea that we *all* have leadership potential, and that different situations invariably require different styles of leadership. Churchill, for example, was widely regarded as a great leader during the Second World War, but somehow his style of leadership worked less well after the war, which was why he was voted out of office.

Anyway, situational leadership maintains that, with any workplace task, whoever's doing that task will have varying levels of aptitude (competence) and attitude (commitment), and so a good leader needs to be able to adapt their leadership style accordingly. If someone is new to their job, for example, they may well have *low aptitude + high attitude* because they don't know what to do, yet they're very keen to learn. In this situation, that person will probably need plenty of **direction** and guidance. Alternatively, if someone's doing a task they've done a zillion times before, and excel at, they may well have *high aptitude* + *high attitude* so, in this situation, it would make sense to **delegate**, and ask how they're getting on from time to time.

The point is, each situation requires a different form of leadership. If a leader is too hands-off with someone who requires lots of direction, they'll feel abandoned and thrown in at the deep end; but, if a leader is too hands-on with someone who needs to be delegated to, they'll feel micro-managed and disempowered.

USEFUL TIPS AND ESCAPE STRATEGIES

If you want to **UP!** your leadership skills, here are three practical tips and strategies that may help:

1 DEVELOP SELF-AWARENESS

Back in the early 1900s – when autocratic leadership was the norm, and the scientific management of Taylorism prevailed – self-awareness wasn't exactly top of the agenda.

Leaders were there to give instructions, and employees were there to carry them out.

As we highlighted a moment ago, however, in the modern goldfish bowl world in which we live, business leaders increasingly need strong people skills (to help inspire, influence and foster innovation). Or, to use academic-speak, they not only need transactional leadership skills, they also need transformational leadership skills, too.

Evidence suggests, however, that one of the best ways to **UP!** our people skills is simply to **UP!** our self-awareness.

Professor Rob Goffee and Professor Gareth Jones of the London Business School, for example, spent years researching what makes great leaders great, and finally came to the conclusion:

'Leadership begins with you – and you will not succeed as a leader unless you have some sense of who you are'

More to the point, in their book *Why Should Anyone be Led by You?*, they go on to say that the secret of leadership is to 'be yourself, more … with skill'.

In other words, self-awareness is not something we do only once, and then move on. Far from it.

As Professor Graham Ward (adjunct professor leadership and coaching at INSEAD) recently told me: 'Great leadership is a lifelong process of self-development and self-management … Put simply, if you don't do the work on yourself you'll be outdistanced by those that do.'

2 LEAD BY EXAMPLE

If there's one thing that's more likely to burst the balloon of inspirational leadership (more than anything else) it's hypocrisy.

That's to say, people at work often despise 'Do as I say, not as I do' leadership.

If you saunter up at your annual conference, for example, ready to give a talk on why business is tough at the moment (and why managerial bonuses need to be suspended for the time being), but then park your brand new and ludicrously expensive car directly in front of the venue, what sort of message is that likely to send out?

Similarly, if you go around telling everyone how you have an open-door policy (but then bite the head off anyone who dares to come to see you), it won't take long for that open-door policy to lose its currency.

Please be aware that recent times have seen the rise of what's called **authentic** leadership – i.e. the appeal of the real – so make sure that what you say to your employees (your social message), and what you really mean (your psychological message), are one and the same thing.

3 LOVE YOUR PEOPLE

Forgive me if this one sounds a bit clutzy, but the point's an important one.

Not long ago I was chatting to Major-General Jonathan Shaw (a former head of the UK's Special Forces) at Oxford University who'd been giving a talk on leadership.

One of his key messages was how – if you want to be an inspirational leader – you need to have a genuine love for your people, and not just focus on the bottom line because, if you can get the people bit right, the figures will follow.

'Leadership', as he said, is fundamentally about 'being creative with people'.

Inspirational leaders are those who genuinely care about their people, and take pride in helping their people to achieve more, for, as Peter Drucker once said:

'Leadership is lifting a person's vision to higher sights, the raising of a person's performance to a higher standard, and the building of a personality beyond its normal limitations'

BUSINESS GENIUS IN ACTION: NEXT STEPS ...

In summary, if you want to **UP!** your leadership skills, here's how:

❶ **P**inpoint how inspirational leadership is as much about what you *don't do*, as what you *do* (from *not* micro-managing, to *not* credit stealing, and *not* crushing creativity to *not* talking defeat).

❷ **I**nvestigate positive role models of leaders (to discover the secrets that have helped them to excel in bringing others with them).

❸ **L**everage the power of direction (for, as Khoi Tu makes clear, leaders can easily lose followers if they're unsure about where they are now, where they are going, why they are going there, and how they will get there).

❹ **O**rchestrate a plan for improving and developing your self-awareness (because self-awareness never really stops and, as Professor Graham Ward points out: 'If you don't do the work on yourself, you'll be outdistanced by those who do').

⑤ **T**arget lifting people's vision to higher sights (by taking a genuine interest in your people and empowering them to stretch beyond the ordinary to achieve the extraordinary).

UP!SPIRATION

'As we all look ahead to the next century, leaders will be those who empower others.'

Bill Gates (founder of Microsoft)

HOW HIGH? HOW FAR?

JOHN D. ROCKEFELLER
(1839 – 1937)

Up until this point, this book has focused almost exclusively on the *positive* side of **UP!**

Now, though, to help you **UP!** your business thinking even further, let's take a quick look at the *flipside*, too.

You know what I mean.

The side where **Business Geniuses** occasionally go too far; the side where **Business Geniuses** end up crossing the line between *exceeding* and *excess.*

So here goes.

Here are the **seven excesses** to watch out for, especially if – as the business author Rob Parsons champions – your ultimate goal is to 'make it in business without losing in life'.

1 EXCESSIVE EFFICIENCY

Improved efficiency is, and always has been, highly prized in the world of business.

After all, it's what drives managers to achieve more with less: airport queues to become shorter, slow IT systems to become faster, and deliveries to be on time.

But what happens when **Business Geniuses** become *too* efficient?

Well, that's when they become *heartless*. Or, to put it another way, so *ambitious* – in their quest to maximise output and minimise resources – their ambition spills into *ruthlessness*. Gengis Khan, for example, was 'damned efficient' (as the Australian billionaire Kerry Packer once remarked), but he wasn't 'exactly loveable'. So let's look at John D. Rockefeller, the founder of Standard Oil, as a case in point.

Rockefeller – according to author Stephen Howarth – started out as a 'humble clerk and book keeper'. But, owing to his ruthless efficiency (i.e. careful accounting + merciless methods), he not only became the owner of Standard Oil, based in Ohio, he also became the richest man in history (i.e. 20 times richer than Bill Gates!).

But at what cost? Evidently, the 'good sweating' he used to give his competitors – until they either went bust or sold to him – prompted suicides and left families destitute along the way. Now, admittedly, in later years Rockefeller did manage to redeem himself somewhat by giving $500 million of his own money to philanthropic causes, but, here's a thought. Shortly before he died in 1937 he said to Henry Ford, 'I'll see you in heaven,' to which Ford allegedly replied, 'If you get in.'

HOW TO AVOID IT

If you want to avoid **excessive efficiency**, keep reminding yourself that it's perfectly OK to strive for excellence in business, yet also remember (as the former New York Mayor Rudolph Giuliani advises in his book *Leadership*) to 'retain your humanity', too.

2 EXCESSIVE ENRICHMENT

Money matters.

We all know that – whatever our profession, and whatever our personal politics – and, though it can't always buy us happiness, it can often bring us 'a more pleasant form of misery' (as the comedian Spike Milligan used to say).

But what happens when money starts to matter *too* much?

Well, that's when *healthy enrichment* (which allows us to support ourselves and our families) can suddenly morph into the Gordon Gekko world of *greed*!

Look at the Spanish Conquistadors, for example, who set off to find El Dorado in the 1500s.

Evidently, according to the historian Michael Wood in his book *Conquistadors*, Hernán Cortés was already 'one of the richest men in Cuba' *before* he headed off to plunder the home of the Aztecs, in modern-day Mexico. Similarly, his fellow opportunist Francisco Pizarro wasn't exactly short of a few bob, either, when he set off to ravage the riches of the Incas, in modern-day Peru.

But to Cortés, Pizarro, and their well-armed motley crew, they wanted more! *Much more!* And this is why – according to Wood – the head of the Incas astutely observed: 'Even if all the snow in the Andes turned to gold, still they would not be satisfied.'

HOW TO AVOID IT

Cultivate the art of *chisoku* (a word I first came across in a book on Zen called *The Ring of the Way* by Taisen Deshimaru). It basically means **to know when enough is enough** because, without *chisoku*, we will never be content, even if we sleep in great palaces. Or, as Deshimaru makes clear: 'Whoever is not satisfied will always feel poor, even if he is rich.'

3 EXCESSIVE EGO

If it wasn't for ego, many of the world's top businesses wouldn't exist today, and most of the world's highest skyscrapers would never have been built.

But, what happens if a person's ego begins to balloon beyond all proportion?

Well, that's when they can become egotistical.

In the movie *Gambit*, for example (the remake of the 1966 classic), a photo of the billionaire Lord Shahbandar – played by Alan Rickman – can be seen on a giant billboard, proudly clutching his new autobiography.

And what's the book called? It's simply called …

Me!

And this says it all, really.

Egotists put themselves at the centre of the universe and choose to forget that 'the self-made success story is a myth', as Professor John Adair makes clear: 'We all depend on others, as they do on us.'

Having said this, however, before we rush to judge narcissists (who have been ever-present since the time of Rameses II, if not before) here's a thought: it's tempting to assume that people in business with massive egos simply love themselves too much. In clinical psychotherapy, however, it seems that the complete opposite is much closer to the truth. People with massive egos *don't* love themselves enough, and that's the problem. They're forever trying to compensate for an emptiness they feel on the inside, which is why they constantly crave attention, adulation and achievements (i.e. trophies) to bolster their fragile self-esteem.

HOW TO AVOID IT

To avoid **excessive ego** we need to *ground* ourselves by remembering we all have feet of clay. Besides, if the statue of Colossus in Rhodes (which was one of the Wonders of the Ancient World) could collapse in 224 BC following an earthquake, and Barings Bank (founded in 1762) could collapse in 1995 following the rogue trading of Nick Leeson, maybe we're not so high and mighty after all.

Linked to this, better to strive for the *confident humility* of someone like Warren Buffet, who, in spite of his phenomenal achievements in business, he appears to have resisted the urge to '**e**dge **g**ood **o**ut'.

4 EXCESSIVE ENTHUSIASM

Ralph Waldo Emerson (American poet, essayist and philosopher) once said, 'Nothing great was ever achieved without enthusiasm.'

What happens, however, if business professionals become over-enthusiastic?

Well, that's when they can become *deluded*.

Just look at what happened on 24 January 1848, for example, when James W. Marshall spotted a few little flecks of gold in Coloma, California. It sparked a Gold Rush in which thousands upon thousands of over-enthusiastic people left everything behind (including their wives and children, sometimes) in search of a treasure most of them never found.

Or think of Greek mythology and the story of Icarus, who became so enthusiastic about flying up, up and away (with the feathered wings his father Daedalus had made him), he ignored warning after warning that the wax on the wings would melt if he flew too close to the sun!

Or how about Captain Ahab – in Melville's *Moby Dick* – whose unrelenting enthusiasm to catch the whale (that had gobbled up his arm in a previous attack) sent him on a monomaniacal quest to find it, leading to the eventual destruction of himself, his boat the *Pequod*, and most of his crew.

So, please note that, although enthusiasm is an essential part of **Business Genius**, we need to ensure we keep a sense of perspective, too. If we don't, we can become gung-ho (i.e. wreckless with our risk-taking) or, in tougher times, even develop a bunker mindset (i.e. tell everyone to move the armies when there are no armies to be moved).

HOW TO AVOID IT

If you want to avoid **excessive enthusiasm**, remember that *big dreams* (unaccompanied by reality) amount to little more than *delusions*.

So strive to get the best of both worlds and – as Covey used to say – be sure that as you climb your ladder of success, it's propped up against the right wall!

5 EXCESSIVE ENCROACHMENT

The world of business has always had its fair share of empire-builders (including the East India Trading Company, which used to account for about 50 per cent of the world's trade).

But what happens when encroachment and conquering goes too far?

Well, that's when some **Geniuses** can end up so busy conquering that they've almost forgotten what they're conquering for.

Look at Alexander the Great, for example. By the age of just 25, he'd succeeded in expanding the Macedonian frontier beyond all recognition, and ruled an Empire stretching 6,000 miles! Added to that, he even ordered 70 different cities to be named after himself (and, yes, **the seven excesses** can overlap!). Yet, how many times did he visit Athens in his lifetime? *Once!*

Or how about Cecil Rhodes (1853–1902), the famous founder of the De Beers diamond business? Rhodes's megalomaniac ambition was not only to build a vast railway from Capetown to Cairo, he even once said: 'I would annexe the planets if I could!'

HOW TO AVOID IT

If you want to avoid **excessive encroachment**, don't just focus on *what* you're doing, keep reminding yourself *why* you're doing it, too (because, as Jim Collins writes in his book *How the Mighty Fall*, many organisations lose sight of that).

For, if the real *why* is not just to conquer and annexe more and more resources through hostile takeovers, etc. but to leave a more meaningful legacy, there are plenty of decent ways of achieving that.

6 EXCESSIVE ELASTICITY

I've long been a champion of lateral thinking in business and the huge commercial and performance improvement benefits it can bring.

But what happens when **Business Geniuses** start to become too lateral or too elastic with their cunningly clever bending of the rules?

Well, that's when decent **Business Genius** soon spills into dodgy **Business Genius**, where countless people from the Great Gatsby to Robert Maxwell, and Bernie Madoff to the former Tour de France champion Lance Armstrong forget to let their conscience be their guide.

And then, of course, there's Enron, who took elasticity to a totally different level with what's considered to be 'The No. 1 white-collar crime of all time' ...

Now the story of how America's seventh largest company (that was once worth $70 billion) collapsed in 2001 is so well documented it's barely worth repeating.

But here's a bizarre twist.

Most organisations get heavily criticised for *not* living up to the promise of their vision statement or catchy strapline. Enron's problem, however, was that they did! And what was their strapline? 'Endless possibilities'.

HOW TO AVOID IT

If you want to avoid **excessive elasticity**, keep reminding yourself that some sacrifices in business (such as Bill Gates reputedly never taking a day off work for the whole of his 20s to help build Microsoft, as referred to earlier) may well be worth it, but sacrificing your integrity seldom is. For as the **Business Genius** Oprah Winfrey once said: 'Real integrity is doing the right thing, knowing that nobody's going to know whether you did or not.'

7 EXCESSIVE ENVY

Finally, let's take a quick look at **excessive envy**.

Let's face it, there's nothing wrong with a bit of friendly rivalry or healthy competition in business. But what happens when it goes too far?

Well, we only have to look at the experiences of Michelangelo to find out.

According to the author Bruno Nardini in his book *Michelangelo: Biography of a Genius*, Michelangelo's arch-rival Bramante was deeply jealous of his talent and success. In fact, so much so that Bramante was the one who suggested to Pope Julius II that Michelangelo should be the one to paint the ceiling of the Sistine Chapel. Why? Because Michelangelo was first and foremost a sculptor, not a painter, and so Bramante thought that by luring him 'into an art that was not his' it would *humiliate* him by forcing him to produce something mediocre.

As it happened, however, half-way through the process, Michelangelo stunned everyone – especially Bramante – by revealing the progress he had made. Although it was still unfinished, everyone could see it was a work of **Genius**; Michelangelo was now not only 'the greatest sculptor of the age', but also fast becoming the 'greatest painter of the age', too.

But was that the end of it? Was Bramante's reaction respect or admiration? Nope. Far from it. The envy just got worse. Bramante even 'tried to persuade the Pope to commission Raphael to paint the other half of the vault'; anything … everything … to make sure that Michelangelo didn't get any more praise or recognition.

HOW TO AVOID IT

If you want to avoid **excessive envy** (or *professional jealousy*, as it's frequently referred to), learn to value who you are. That way, you'll learn to become more generous spirited, and feel enriched by the achievements of others, rather than feeling threatened by them. More importantly, however, you'll have become what Alfred Lord Tennyson called an *intelligent merchant* because 'No man ever got very high by pulling other people down.'

So, there you have it.

Yes, of course these seven excesses aren't the only excesses but, hopefully – in a book this size – they'll do for now.

OK, let's now quickly move on to three final **UP!lifting** points.

POINT 1 BUSINESS GENIUS DOESN'T ALWAYS HAVE TO BE COMPLICATED

On the contrary. As we touched on earlier, **Business Genius** is all about **the triple S of business success.** In other words:

Seeing things differently

Like how Jeff Bezos noticed that internet growth was growing exponentially back in the 1990s, and promptly left his day-to-day Wall Street computer analyst job to set up Amazon.

Or like André and Edouard Michelin (who provided farming equipment in France back in the late 1880s) who noticed how long it took for the glue to harden after they repaired the punctured tyres of a wandering cyclist, and promptly went on to develop 'a detachable pneumatic tyre that could be repaired in just 15 minutes', which revolutionised the worldwide transport industry (source: *Superbrands*).

Strategising differently

Like Josiah Wedgwood, who back in the mid-1700s found that his plan to become a thrower in a Staffordshire pottery was smashed to smithereens when he tragically had a leg amputed following an illness.

But did he quit? No. He came up with a smarter strategy and decided to become a modeller instead (which didn't involve him having to stand around all the time). As a result, Wedgwood went on to discover highly innovative ways of making ceramics, and his china became famous all over the globe.

Striving differently

Like Irving Berlin (the **Genius** composer of *White Christmas*) who strongly believed that 'Talent is just the start'.

Like the industrious Arnold Schwarzenegger who once said, 'You can't climb the ladder of success with your hands in your pocket.'

Or like the legendary film producer George Lucas who stated: 'Working hard is very important. You're not going to get anywhere without working extremely hard.'

POINT 2 BUSINESS GENIUS DOESN'T ALWAYS HAVE TO BE 'BIG'

Again, on the contrary.

More often than not it's the *micro-improvements* in our business thinking, and business behaviours, that can make all the difference.

For example:

→ Think of the **Business Genius** Kirkpatrick MacMillan who, back in 1839, came up with the deceptively simple idea of adding pedals to bicycles.

→ Think of the **Business Genius** Mary Anderson who, back in 1903, came up with the deceptively simple idea of adding windscreen wipers to car windows.

→ Think of the **Business Genius** creative team at Saatchi & Saatchi, back in 1973, who came up with the deceptively simple idea of using one word – 'probably' – to help sell beer, inspiring the infamous slogan: 'Carlsberg … *Probably* the best lager in the world', which became one of the most successful slogans of all time, and ended up being used continuously for the next 38 years!

POINT 3 BUSINESS GENIUS DOESN'T ALWAYS HAVE TO BE DULL

'Creativity is intelligence having fun.'
Albert Einstein (theoretical physicist)

CONCLUSION: UPWARDS AND ONWARDS . . .

'The shell must break before the bird can fly.'
Alfred Lord Tennyson (Poet Laureate)

The aim of this book has been to highlight how **Business Genius** is – above all else – an **altitude of mind** ...

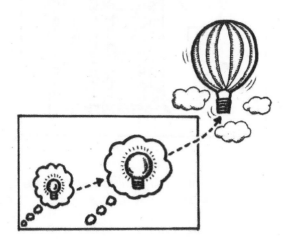

... And this altitude (as we've explored throughout) is built upon us **seeing** things differently, **strategising** differently and **striving** differently.

With this in mind, whatever line of work you're in, I hope it will inspire you upwards and onwards to achieve even greater levels of success, both personally and professionally.

After all, as Einstein once said:

'Logic will get you from A to B ...

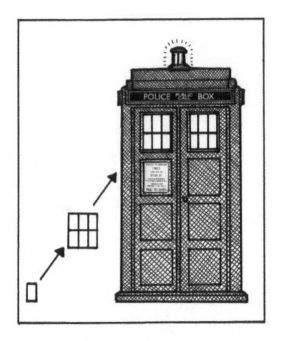

... Imagination will take you everywhere'

FURTHER INFORMATION

Originally, I was planning to write a comprehensive list of references for this book. As you can probably imagine, however, we'd have had such a mountain of data that it might have ended up being longer than the book itself.

With this in mind, if you'd like further information on **Business Genius**, I'd strongly recommend you read publications by any, or all, of the authors I've mentioned along the way …

AND FINALLY

You may also want to visit www.geniusthinking.co.uk or www.jamesbannerman.com to explore a wide range of business consulting, training and coaching services for helping you to boost your personal and professional success.

What did you think of this book?

We're really keen to hear from you about this book, so that we can make our publishing even better.

Please log on to the following website and leave us your feedback.

It will only take a few minutes and your thoughts are invaluable to us.

www.pearsoned.co.uk/bookfeedback

INDEX